# Social and Personality Development

*Social and Personality Development* looks at the processes by which we come to be who we are. It covers a range of topics central to personality and developmental psychology. The book is arranged in three sections, the first covering the main theories of personality, the second describing the development of gender and the third focusing on adolescence. It is suitable for the AQA-A A2 Level examination, but will also be of interest to those studying education, nursing and other related disciplines.

**Tina Abbott** is an experienced A-level teacher and examiner and is an executive member of the Association for the Teaching of Psychology.

# Routledge Modular Psychology

*Series editors*: Cara Flanagan is a Reviser for AS and A2 level Psychology and lectures at Inverness College. Philip Banyard is Associate Senior Lecturer in Psychology at Nottingham Trent University and a Chief Examiner for AS and A2 level Psychology. Both are experienced writers.

The *Routledge Modular Psychology* series is a completely new approach to introductory-level psychology, tailor-made to the new modular style of teaching. Each short book covers a topic in more detail than any large textbook can, allowing teacher and student to select material exactly to suit any particular course or project.

The books have been written especially for those students new to higher-level study, whether at school, college or university. They include specially designed features to help with technique, such as a model essay at an average level with an examiner's comments to show how extra marks can be gained. The authors are all examiners and teachers at the introductory level.

The *Routledge Modular Psychology* texts are all user-friendly and accessible and include the following features:

- practice essays with specialist commentary to show how to achieve a higher grade
- chapter summaries to assist with revision
- progress and review exercises
- glossary of key terms
- summaries of key research
- further reading to stimulate ongoing study and research
- cross-referencing to other books in the series

*Also available in this series (titles listed by syllabus section):*

To Little Tina and Beans,
Love and Peace

# Social and Personality Development

*Tina Abbott*

First published 2001
by Routledge
27 Church Road, Hove, East Sussex BN3 2FA

Simultaneously published in the USA and Canada
by Taylor and Francis Inc.
29 West 35th Street, New York NY 10001

*Routledge is an imprint of the Taylor and Francis Group*

© 2001 Tina Abbott

Typeset in Times and Frutiger by Keystroke,
Jacaranda Lodge, Wolverhampton
Printed and bound in Great Britain by
TJ International Ltd, Padstow, Cornwall

Cover design by Terry Foley

*British Library Cataloguing in Publication Data*
A catalogue record for this book is available from the British Library

*Library of Congress Cataloging-in-Publication Data*
Abbott, Tina, 1961–
    Social and personality development / Tina Abbott.
        p. cm. — (Routledge modular psychology)
    Includes bibliographical references and index.
    ISBN 0-415-23103-5 (hbk) — isbn 0-415-23104-3 (pbk.)
1. Personality development. 2. Gender identity. 3. Adolescent psychology.
I. Title. II. Series
BF723. P4 A23 2001
155.2'5—dc21                                                     2001034799

ISBN 0–415–23103–5 (hbk)
ISBN 0–415–23104–3 (pbk)

# Contents

# Illustrations

**Figures**

## Tables

# Acknowledgements

The series editor and Routledge acknowledge the expert help of Paul Humphreys, Examiner and Reviser for AS and A2 level Psychology, in compiling the Study aids chapter of each book in the series.

AQA (AEB) examination questions are reproduced by permission of the Assessment and Qualifications Alliance. The AQA do not accept responsibility for the answers or examiner comments in the Study aids chapter of this book or any other in the series.

The author would like to thank Adrian for the love, support and guidance he has given her during the writing of this book. She would also like to thank her sons Josh and Finn for their patience and understanding, and Warrington for his friendship.

# Introduction

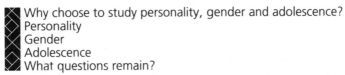

Why choose to study personality, gender and adolescence?
Personality
Gender
Adolescence
What questions remain?

## Why choose to study personality, gender and adolescence?

The purpose of this book is to introduce the reader to a variety of traditional and contemporary psychological theories and studies, which play a key role in informing our understanding of the individual. The three areas covered: personality, gender and adolescence, represent core aspects of individual development. These aspects not only play a profound role in shaping the people we eventually become, but continue to impact on us throughout our lives.

The book is divided into three sections: personality development, gender development and adolescence.

## Personality

The study of personality has a long history. From the ideas of philosophers such as Galen (second century AD), who believed our personalities are influenced by the presence of bodily fluids (see Chapter 3), we move to contemporary psychologists, some of whom focus on internal characteristics, such as traits or instincts, while others see external factors in the environment, as important in influencing the ways we behave and therefore our personalities.

The first section of this book focuses on the key approaches to the study of personality, including the ideas of theorists such as Hans Eysenck and Gordon Allport, who see personality as continually influenced by permanent traits, that may or may not be unique to the individual. These theorists have taken a psychometric approach by devising questionnaires that can be used to measure personality. Social learning theorists, such as Albert Bandura and Walter Mischel, who oppose the permanency of personality put forward by psychometric theorists, believe instead that personality is simply a result of learning in a variety of social situations, and therefore is flexible and changeable. Last in this section is the psychoanalytic approach (sometimes referred to as the psychodynamic approach), focusing mainly on its founder, Sigmund Freud, who argued that behaviour, and therefore personality, is driven by dynamic inner forces such as needs, desires and beliefs. Psychodynamic theorists and social learning theorists share a common belief in the flexibility of human personality. Their differences however are reflected in the therapeutic approaches they advocate. Whereas social learning theorists believe behaviour change can best be achieved using behaviourist strategies such as positive or negative reinforcement (see Chapter 5), psychoanalysts believe more in the power of therapeutic interventions that act to unearth repressed memories with the aid of techniques such as free association (see Chapter 4).

Collectively, these approaches to the study of personality provide us with a complex and sometimes contradictory view of the individual, that can raise interesting questions and debates about the nature of human personality, informing our understanding, and hopefully leading us to greater insight.

## Gender

As we strive to reach an understanding of the individual through the study of human personality, we cannot fail to realise the crucial role played by gender. Whatever situation we find ourselves in, whether through work or play, our gender is usually salient. That is to say we are often made aware of our maleness or our femaleness through the options available to us, and the choices we are sometimes compelled to make. For example, in terms of family, work and/or education, gender is often the key aspect that guides our decisions. Do we want a family? Or would we like to pursue a career first? Are we prepared to travel with our work? And where do we see ourselves in five years time? The answers to these questions are often heavily influenced by our gender.

Some people may argue that in contemporary society, gender no longer has the impact that it traditionally had. Females are no longer expected to stay at home and look after the family, while the role of males as main provider is fast changing. Careers are available to both genders if they wish to pursue them, and carers of children these days are often male. But despite these changes it is easy to see that inequality between the genders still exists. If a female does decide on a career rather than a family, she may still be stigmatised for her unwillingness to have children. On the other hand, a male who decides to stay at home and take care of the family may be seen as inadequate in some way. For example, he may be viewed as lacking the characteristics that make a 'man', such as the power and ambition to succeed in a career. From a very young age differences between the genders are continually reinforced, from the clothes we wear, the toys we are encouraged to play with, and even the names we are given. Our parents, teachers, peers, the media, books we read, stories we hear, almost every aspect of our social life is geared towards this difference. Therefore gender is a constant contributor to the person we are, and the study of gender is essential to our understanding of personality.

## Adolescence

The final section of this book focuses on a part of our life that incurs a lot of change and upheaval: adolescence. It is during this time that we begin to question what we want out of life, and to grapple with some major life issues such as identity and sexuality. For some teenagers adolescence can be a particularly tough and demanding time. All kinds of influences play a part in aiding the process or making life hard for the young person. Parents, peers and teachers have an influence, often in conflict with social messages fed through the media. All can provide support and motivation, or, equally, cause distress and despair.

Throughout this section of the book we focus on the various ways that teenagers react and interact at home, at school or work, and with friends and family as they strive towards adulthood. We also look at specific incidences that can occur during this time, such as adolescent pregnancy, eating disorders and suicide. We look at the ways society can support young people through the agency of social policy, and consider why harmful incidences such as teenage pregnancies, suicide and eating disorders are on the increase in some Western societies. We discuss both the social and personal factors that may be impacting on this, and the implications for society as a whole.

## What questions remain?

Of course there are many more questions that remain unanswered and even unasked. The diversity and complexity of human behaviour will I hope continue to provoke us to search for new explanations and insights into the underlying basis of personality. Along with the impact of adolescence and gender on the behaviours and personalities of individuals, other major life events have as much, if not more of an influence on who we are as people. The arrival of adulthood, promotion at work, a term of imprisonment, the birth of a child: all of these occurrences can change our outlook on life and so affect our personalities.

In writing this book, my aim has been to provide an understanding of some of the factors that help to shape us into the people we become. I hope it will ignite in the reader a curiosity about the causes of human behaviour and the way in which an understanding of this, through the study of psychology, can be used to improve the quality of our lives.

## Further Reading

Eysenck, M.W. (2000) *Psychology: A student's handbook*, Hove, UK: Psychology Press. An excellent general textbook that provides a good grounding in approaches to the study of personality, as well as interesting ideas on adolescence and gender development.

Sampson, E.E. (1991) *Social Worlds, Personal Lives: An introduction to Social Psychology*, New York: Harcourt, Brace, Jovanovich. Provides in-depth coverage of research on personality development.

# Section I

## PERSONALITY DEVELOPMENT

# 2

# Two approaches to the study of personality

The study of personality
Idiographic and nomothetic approaches
Advantage and disadvantages
Conclusion
Summary

## The study of personality

Personality is a concept used in everyday life to describe the character of a person. It is often seen as an unchanging part of their makeup. A commonsense approach to the study of personality might include the use of everyday language to identify certain characteristics. For example an individual might be described as very *outgoing* and *self-confident*, easily able to deal with people and situations. Or they might be described as *shy* and *withdrawn*, finding it difficult to interact socially. A person might be admired for their wit and charm, or they may be disliked for their coldness and aloofness. These ways of describing people are commonly employed in western cultures.

As individuals negotiate their way through life, success often depends on how they respond to others, as they participate in the give and take of communication. We often categorise ourselves and others as certain personality types, in order to predict whether the outcome of a particular social situation is likely to be successful or not. It appears we find it useful to categorise people in this way, in order to give us a better understanding of each other's behaviour.

So how does this way of defining people differ from the way psychologists have tried to understand and study personality?

## Defining personality

A number of psychologists have attempted to define this **hypothetical construct** we call personality. Having a definition helps to provide a starting point from which to develop theories of personality more fully. These theories can then be usefully applied to real life situations, for example in advising parents on positive ways of interacting with their children, in line with their individual personalities, or by constructing more effective ways of treating specific mental disorders (such as obsessive behaviours).

However, because of the diversity of theories that have sprung up in the area of personality, there doesn't exist one formal definition. The meaning of personality has become tied to the underlying perspective of the theorist. For example **constructionists** such as Hampson (1995) see personality as 'constructed in the course of social interaction from a person's self presentation, the perception of this presentation by an audience, and self-awareness'. Whereas **humanists** such as Rogers (1951) see personality as grounded in the way we experience ourselves as people, and which particular characteristics make us distinctly human.

An important difference between various approaches to the study of personality is that while some theorists assume people *possess* a personality (they were born that way, or they are predisposed to behave in a certain way due to their biology or genes), others have developed the idea that people simply *manifest* behaviours that are brought about by the situation they find themselves in. Both approaches may incorporate the language of personality types or personality traits. However, a simple definition that would suit both approaches might be: *the behaviour a person exhibits at any given time in their lives*.

## The value of studying personality

The study of personality is linked with many other areas of research within psychology, such as investigations into perception, stereotyping and the self-concept. For example, the area of perception is concerned with how the individual reacts to the world around them. A very outgoing, sociable individual may perceive the world as an adventurous place full of interest and intrigue, whereas a shy and retiring individual may perceive the world as a dangerous and threatening place. The way we perceive the world is therefore in some way shaped by how we perceive ourselves. This self-perception (or self-concept) comes about from a variety of factors, but is often formed by the language either we or others use to describe us, thereby categorising us as a particular kind of person. The study of personality, therefore, can be helpful in understanding not only the characteristics of human nature but can also shed light on other psychological phenomena.

## Idiographic and nomothetic approaches

Historically, research into personality has tended to be split between two approaches: the **idiographic** approach and the **nomothetic** approach. This division reflects an important difference of opinion in the way psychologists view people as the subject matter. When studied idiographically people are seen as unique individuals, whereas taking a nomothetic approach assumes that people are essentially similar and share characteristics with each other. The difference between these two approaches is discussed in more detail below.

### *Idiographic approaches*

The *idiographic* approach (from the Greek 'idios' meaning personal or private) takes the view that we are unique individuals and should be studied as such. This means that we cannot rely on descriptions of common behaviours to describe certain types of people, such as people who are shy or people who are aggressive, but should treat each person as uniquely different from any other.

So how can this approach be applied to the study of personality? Taking a purely idiographic approach would require a detailed analysis of an individual's thoughts, feelings and behaviours, and would not assume that the resulting profile could be applied to anybody else. The idea of universal features or general behaviours put forward to explain human behaviour does not belong to, and is not the language of an idiographic approach.

The main advocates of the idiographic approach are from the humanistic school of thought. This school includes prominent theorists such as Carl Rogers who took a person-centred approach to therapy, George Kelly who developed the personal construct theory, and Gordon Allport (whose personality theory we will discuss in Chapter 3) who described people as possessing 'unique personal characteristics'. Sigmund Freud was another theorist who took an idiographic approach, by focusing on the individual as the main unit of study. Freud's personality theory was developed from case studies of his patients. A final example is Eric Erikson, who put forward a whole life theory of psychosocial stages, through which each person must pass during their lifetime. Both Freud and Erikson will be discussed in detail later in the book.

To conclude, taking an idiographic approach means researching a theory or phenomena by studying people individually and recognising their uniqueness, without trying to categorise them.

### Nomothetic approaches

The nomothetic approach (from the Greek 'nomos' meaning law) relies on the assumption that we share many characteristics with our fellow human beings, and that the study of behaviours we hold in common will lead to a more useful understanding of people. It is typically characterised by the use of experimental methods, such as measuring individuals on a scale, or carrying out controlled studies where variables can be isolated, in order to uncover universal laws that can be applied to everyone. Taking a nomothetic approach involves categorising people in order to describe or uncover the causes of common behaviours, such as sociability or generosity.

This approach has been employed by cognitive psychologists such as Raymond Cattell and Hans Eysenck, both of whom believe that the basic core of human personality is made up of a number of traits or dimensions. As a well-known example, Eysenck put forward introversion/extroversion as a universal personality dimension that can be employed to describe and measure part of any individual's personality in varying degrees. (Eysenck's theory will be discussed fully in Chapter 3.)

Before reading any further see if in your own words you can explain the difference between idiographic and nomothetic approaches to the study of personality.

Progress exercise

## Advantages and disadvantages

The debate over the use of the two approaches has developed because each approach has both strengths and weaknesses associated with it.

A key strength of the nomothetic approach is that its methodologies are in line with other sciences such as chemistry or physics. These sciences are largely built around the discovery of universal laws which can be used to explain natural phenomena. However, in terms of psychological research, the possibility of uncovering and applying universal 'laws' to people in order to predict their behaviour has a number of problems associated with it. The outcome of such research could lead to unethical consequences if it were used to control and shape people's lives. Historically this has occurred in the use of tests which claimed to measure a universal construct known as intelligence (see Gould 1981), which sadly led to the oppression of minority groups on the basis of their low scores in these tests. A further problem with nomothetic research findings is that they may provide only a superficial understanding of an individual, a particularly worrying weakness in terms of the use of these findings in diagnosing mental disorders. Nevertheless, uncovering universal behaviour patterns for some psychological disorders (such as those exhibited in autism) can provide us with crucial information that may help in constructing positive and effective treatments.

Idiographic studies uncover individual differences and allow us to develop detailed analyses of the individual person. This is where the idiographic approach has a real advantage over the nomothetic approach, as it means that we can tailor diagnosis and treatment much more specifically to meet the needs of the individual. We can also gain a greater insight into an individual's strengths and weaknesses, and so guide them more effectively.

Idiographic research has often been the catalyst that has encouraged further nomothetic investigation into specific areas of interest. One example of this is the work carried out by Jean Piaget on the cognitive development of children. Piaget took an idiographic approach by observing and interviewing individual children over a period of time. From this he developed his influential theory of cognitive development, which sparked off a multitude of nomothetic experimental studies. Another example is the work of Freud, where again his approach was essentially idiographic (i.e. case studies) but led to nomothetic conclusions, such as his suggestion of the existence of universal defence mechanisms (although this theory is difficult to prove empirically). This leads us to the main disadvantage of an idiographic approach: the generation of empirical evidence from individual cases means that we cannot legitimately generalise idiographic findings to all people. The findings are by themselves unreliable because they are based on the subjective experiences or behaviours of a limited number of individuals, and may be invalid if we try to apply them to our understanding of people as a whole.

### Nomothetic versus idiographic

Is the distinction between idiographic and nomothetic approaches really valid? Holt (1967) argues that the whole issue is built on a false dichotomy. To say that an individual should only be studied in terms of what makes him unique, with no reference to universal behaviours (or even other individuals), is an impossibility. As pointed out by Radford and Kirby (1975) 'a truly unique individual would be incomprehensible, in fact not recognizable as an individual'.

However the dichotomy does still stand and has some use, not only in facilitating a discussion between various approaches, but also in ensuring that we continually question what it is to be a person.

## Conclusion

Both the idiographic and nomothetic approaches to the study of personality can be beneficial to our understanding of people. Each approach has its own strengths and its own weaknesses. The view put forward by Kluckhohn and Murray (1953) on the understanding of people is relevant here. They note that every person is like no other,

**Table 2.1** Personality theories categorised as idiographic or nomothetic

|  | Behaviour seen as due to personality traits, where change is unlikely | Behaviour seen as due to environmental factors, where change is possible |
|---|---|---|
| Nomothetic | Eysenck's type theory | |
| | Psychoanalytic theories | |
| Idiographic | Allport's trait theory | Humanistic theories |

Adapted from Gross (1990) by permission of Hodder and Stoughton Educational Limited

like some other and like all other people. In other words there are some similarities and some differences between people within cultures, and between cultures. But also there are some universal characteristics that supersede culture and individual differences. It seems that we must draw on both approaches if we are to achieve a more complete understanding of people.

Draw up a table to show the main advantages and disadvantages of the idiographic and nomothetic approaches to the study of personality. Use examples of research to illustrate your points.

Review exercise

## Summary

Personality is an important everyday concept, helping us to understand the behaviour of others. Research into personality has tended to be split between two approaches: the idiographic approach and the nomothetic approach. The idiographic approach involves studying people as unique individuals. Idiographic studies are well suited to situations where a deep understanding of the individual person is required.

They have also often been the catalyst that has encouraged further nomothetic investigation into specific areas of interest. However, we cannot automatically generalise idiographic findings to all people because they are based on studies of a limited number of individuals. Nomothetic research involves the study of the behaviour of many individuals, typically relying on statistical tests to uncover trends and differences. The nomothetic approach thus complements the idiographic approach and is helpful in studies aimed at firmly establishing universal laws of behaviour. As useful as they are, nomothetic research findings may on their own provide an oversimplified picture of behaviour which is not always useful in practical applications.

## Further reading

Gross, R.D. (1999) *Psychology: The Science of Mind and Behaviour* (third edition), London: Hodder and Stoughton. A detailed discussion of the idiographic/ nomothetic debate linked to the study of personality.

# Trait and type theories

## Introduction

The word **psychometric** originates from the terms 'psycho' referring to mind, and 'metric' meaning measurement, and simply means measurement of the mind, or measurement of an aspect of the mind. Examples include the measurement of intelligence, attitudes and personality, and would typically involve the use of questionnaires or tests.

The two personality theories we will cover in this chapter are Eysenck's type theory, and Allport's trait theory. These theories illustrate different approaches to the study of personality. Both theories were developed using psychometrics, but whereas Eysenck's approach is nomothetic in nature, Allport takes an idiographic approach.

## Eysenck's type theory

Hans Eysenck is the UK's most cited psychologist, and the personality test he developed is still widely used. During the 1940s Eysenck was working in a psychiatric hospital in London. His job was to make an initial assessment of each patient before their mental disorder was clinically diagnosed by a psychiatrist. Eysenck became interested in the idea of comparing the medical diagnosis given to patients with an analysis of their behaviour from a psychological viewpoint. He began to look for a simple method of description that could account for the various patterns of behaviour shown by individual patients.

In order to achieve this Eysenck employed a technique known as **factor analysis**, a statistical method originally devised by Charles Spearman (1904). Spearman's interest was in human intelligence, and his aim was to find a single factor (which he called *g*) that could explain multiple correlations observed for an array of different intelligence tests. Eysenck adapted this idea to show how various behaviour patterns could also be explained by a small number of factors (which he called a dimension). As an example of how this works, imagine we want to find out what factors are involved in determining why people come to like particular pop bands. We might start by asking lots of people to name their favourite band, and then list all the key reasons why they like this band. Once we have collected lots of reasons (or *factors*) we can group similar answers together under separate headings, and it is these headings we call *dimensions*. For example, lots of people may have felt that physical appearance played a key role in why they preferred a particular band. They may have used terms like 'good looking', 'sexy', 'hunky' etc. These terms (or *factors*) can easily be grouped together as the meaning is very similar, and we could call this cluster of factors 'attractiveness'. Therefore the dimension that accounts for these factors would be the *attractiveness* of the lead singer (see Figure 3.1). Another might be the *musical talent* of a band member. So to recap, the technique of factor analysis would isolate those factors that occur in clusters and appear to indicate a trend or common explanation, or as Eysenck called it a dimension. The implications of this might be that, according to this analysis, in order to be popular a band must have an attractive lead singer who also has musical talent.

Eysenck applied this factor analysis technique to the study of 700 battle-fatigued soldiers, who were medically diagnosed as 'neurotic'

| Factors | Dimension |
|---|---|
| Hunky | |
| Sexy | Attractiveness |
| Good-looking | |

*Figure 3.1* Diagram illlustrating factors and resulting dimension

i.e. moody, anxious etc. by the hospital psychiatrists. Eysenck, using the technique of factor analysis, found that their behaviour could be represented using two dimensions, which he called **introversion/extroversion** (E) and **neuroticism/stability** (N). The dimensions were independent or orthogonal from each other and they represented two separate continuums along which individuals could score, rather like co-ordinates on a map. These two dimensions formed the basis of Eysenck's initial personality theory (Eysenck 1947). See Figure 3.2.

The dimensions of personality proposed by Eysenck are similar in some respects to a much earlier 'type' theory. The Greeks believed that

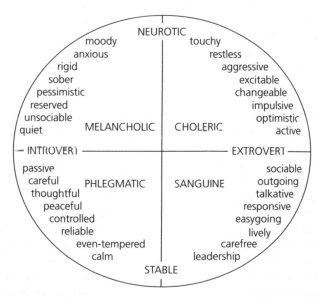

*Figure 3.2* Eysenck's initial theory

our personality is made up of four 'temperaments' (Galen, second century AD). It was thought that these temperaments were influenced by the presence of fluids in the body, and whichever temperament was most prevalent dictated an individual's personality type. The four temperaments were called sanguine (an excess of blood), choleric (an excess of yellow bile), melancholic (an excess of black bile) or phlegmatic (an excess of phlegm). These temperaments describe types or categories of personality. The theory assumed that individuals could only belong to one of the four types.

An important difference between Eysenck's theory and that of the Greeks is that Eysenck's types are made up of a combination of traits. For example an extrovert is a type of personality identified by Eysenck as being based on the observed traits (or factors) of sociability, talkativeness, liveliness and leadership, etc. A neurotic is a type which could be described as anxious, worrying, moody and often depressed.

In addition, Eysenck's types consist of continuums along which individuals can be placed. Therefore a person is not one or the other type, but more or less of a type. For example a person may be described as a 'stable extrovert' or a 'neurotic extrovert' or conversely a 'stable introvert' or a 'neurotic introvert'. Some confusion may arise when we consider that Eysenck's theory is called a type theory, as it does include both type and trait components.

### The final dimension

In 1952 Eysenck proposed a third dimension to his personality theory which he called **psychoticism** (P). (P) represents a further dimension which is unrelated to both (E) and (N), in the same way as they are unrelated to each other. A person scoring high on psychoticism would incorporate risk-taking and impulsiveness as part of their personality characteristics. They may also be described as a loner, lacking in feelings and empathy, cruel and often troublesome. However, unlike extroversion and neuroticism, psychoticism is not evenly distributed throughout the population. Eysenck believes that the type psychoticism is strongly linked with other psychiatric labels such as 'psychopathic', 'schizoid' and 'behavioural disorder'. He stresses however that the dimension of psychoticism is only a predisposition to a psychological disorder, not an actual psychological disorder itself. Others (e.g. Claridge

1967) have suggested that under extreme stress these predispositions can indeed become psychiatric illness.

The features of Eysenck's personality theory that we have discussed so far suggest that Eysenck sees personality as a fixed component of an individual's way of dealing with the world. Whether the person is outgoing and confident, or shy and retiring, they can be categorised according to this theory.

### The use of psychometrics

Initially, Eysenck undertook a lengthy observation of a sample of patients with psychiatric problems in an attempt to assess the personality dimensions apparent in these individuals. However this proved a long and tedious approach, and excluded the application of his personality theory to a wider population. To remedy this Eysenck and his colleagues devised a set of questions to measure the two dimensions of extraversion/introversion and neuroticism/stability that could be easily administered to anyone. The questionnaire, a self-report scale which became known as the EPI (Eysenck's Personality Inventory) (Eysenck and Eysenck 1964), required only simple yes/no answers, and included a built-in 'lie scale' which would assess the individual's tendency to give **socially desirable** answers. These are answers that are culturally desirable to the individual and would lead to a biased self-assessment. (See Table 3.1 for a sample of questions from the EPI.)

The EPI does not however measure the dimension of psychoticism, and later Eysenck developed a further scale known as the EPQ (Eyenck's Personality Questionnaire), (Eysenck and Eysenck 1975) which includes this dimension.

Answer the following questions:

1 Explain the meaning of the term 'psychometrics'.
2 Name the three dimensions of personality put forward by Hans Eysenck.
3 Describe some of the factors that make up the dimension of psychoticism.

Progress exercise

| *Table 3.1* Some questions from Eysenck's Personality Inventory (EPI) | |
| --- | --- |
| Do you prefer to have few but special friends? | Yes/No |
| Do you daydream a lot? | Yes/No |
| When people shout at you do you shout back? | Yes/No |
| Are all your habits good and desirable ones? | Yes/No |
| Do you sometimes gossip? | Yes/No |

### The biological basis of Eysenck's type theory

Having proposed that people can be meaningfully classified into types, Eysenck further suggested that these types have their basis in the physiological makeup of the individual. He related the behaviour of the individual to the functioning of their **autonomic nervous system (ANS)**. The explanation put forward by Eysenck is that the behaviour of an individual (in other words their personality) is dependent in part on the balance between the *excitation* and *inhibition* processes of their nervous system. Put simply, the more sensitive (easily aroused or excitable) a person is the more introverted their personality. This is because they try to avoid over-arousal by being introverted. On the other hand, the less easily aroused a person is, the more extroverted their personality. This is because they try to seek out external stimuli in order to feel some arousal.

Eysenck believed that the neuroticism dimension was also linked to the autonomic nervous system, but this time in terms of how quickly and intensely a person responds to external stressors. When we are faced with a stressful situation, such as having to perform in front of an audience, our ANS is activated and this causes a number of physical reactions to occur. These reactions include, for example, the production of the hormone adrenaline, the speeding up of our heart rate, and the closing down of our digestive system. These responses enable us to face up to the cause of the stress, with all our bodily resources ready for action. In the case of those scoring high on the neuroticism dimension the stress response would be very extreme, as these people tend to overreact to external stressors.

According to Eysenck people with a neurotic personality possess an ANS that reacts much more quickly and more strongly to stress, compared to less emotional and more stable personalities. So this could explain why neurotics may feel stressed more often, and perhaps for longer periods.

With regard to the dimension of psychoticism, Eysenck did not attempt a full biological explanation, other than that he believed a link exists between the behavioural aspects of psychoticism and the release of hormones, particularly male hormones (androgens). However he offered no detailed explanation of how this might work.

### Conditionability

If Eysenck's claims about the biological basis of personality are true, then it should be relatively easy to illustrate this by comparing the levels of **conditionability** between introverts and extroverts. According to Eysenck, introverts should be more easily conditioned using the stimulus response approach than extroverts, as they are more easily aroused and react strongly to external stimuli. However, on reviewing an array of relevant studies, Eysenck found that only 50 per cent of the sample supported his prediction, while the other 50 per cent opposed it.

What were the three personality dimensions put forward by Eysenck?
For each of them, outline the biological processes that are thought to underlie them.

Progress exercise

## Evaluation of Eysenck's theory

The evidence used to test Eysenck's personality theory comes in various forms, including twin studies, clinical trials, and various validity checks. These are summarised below.

### Twin studies

Shields (1976) found that monozygotic (genetically identical) twins were significantly more alike on the dimensions E and P than dizygotic (non-identical) twins, thereby providing some support for Eysenck's biological basis of personality. Other twin studies (e.g. Loehlin, Willerman and Horn 1988) have found that only 50 per cent of the variation of scores on personality dimensions are due to inherited traits, suggesting that biology is not the only explanation, and other factors such as learning must also be considered. Therefore evidence from twin studies is not conclusive.

### Clinical trials

Trials using psychiatric patients have shown that individuals who score high on the neuroticism dimension typically exhibit a wide variety of ANS responses. Patients sometimes reacted very quickly to stressors as Eysenck predicted, but at other times they were very slow to respond. They also typically failed to habituate (become used to and cease to respond) to continued external stimuli (Lader 1975). Both results imply that their ANS's are functioning poorly, rather than extra sensitively, as Eysenck proposed.

### Laboratory studies

Eysenck's theory predicts that introverts will exhibit higher levels of physiological arousal than extroverts. This can be measured with an apparatus known as a polygram that simultaneously records various measures such as heart rate, blood pressure, galvanic skin response and pulse rate. Gale (1981) reviewed the findings of thirty studies that had attempted to find a correlation between personality scores and heightened arousal. Approximately 50 per cent of these studies showed a positive correlation with significant differences between extraverts and introverts. More recent studies have obtained a higher percentage of correlation, although Gale argues that the presence of an experimenter and the environment in which the studies take place, could influence the responses of introverts much more than that of extroverts. This may invalidate the findings of these studies.

### Validity checks

So far we have looked at the evidence provided by various studies that have attempted to prove or disprove Eysenck's theory of personality.

However because Eysenck's theory relies on the use of a questionnaire to categorise individuals, it makes sense to also examine whether his questionnaire actually measures what it purports to measure. This is known as testing the **validity** of the questionnaire. There are many different types of validity and in this section we will consider a variety of different types.

*Construct validity* is the primary form of validation used by trait theorists, and, put simply, it looks at the relationship between the test and the various behaviours the theory predicts. For example, individuals identified as extraverts are predicted as being outgoing and sociable and this should become apparent in the test. In this way the usefulness of the theory is evaluated.

Furnham (1981) conducted a study on the leisure activities chosen by individuals who had been assessed using Eysenck's Personality Questionnaire (EPQ). He found the EPQ to be a good indicator of behaviour, with individuals identified as extraverts preferring stimulating social activities involving competitiveness and assertiveness, those identified as neurotics avoiding activities involving social interaction, and subjects who scored highly on psychoticism preferring situations where they could manipulate others. This shows that in this particular study the EPQ has construct validity.

A different type of validity is known as *predictive validity*. A check for this may be employed whenever tests are used to make predictions about behaviour. Eysenck and Eysenck (1985) using the EPQ in the initial assessment, found that in comparison with subjects identified as introverts, those classified as extraverts actually changed jobs more frequently, had more sexual partners, and were more likely to divorce. Therefore, in this instance, Eysenck's prediction that extraverts are sensation seekers appears to be validated.

A further type of validity worth considering is *concurrent validity*. A check for this involves comparisons of the results of an existing test with those of a new test, to see if a correlation between them exists. Eysenck attempted to provide evidence of concurrent validity by administering his questionnaire to an experimental group of people who had all been diagnosed as suffering from the same condition (i.e. neuroticism), and to a control group. He found a significant difference in scores between the two groups, with the experimental group much more likely to score highly on the neuroticism dimension. This suggests that the scales do appear to provide concurrent validity.

Further work by Gibson (1976) developed these findings by looking at the *consensual validity* of the EPI. This is assessed when the items (questions) that form the questionnaire are tested for their objectivity in assessing the individual. Gibson undertook this by asking students to rate a group of their friends using the EPI, and then by asking the group of friends to rate themselves. He found that the ratings of the friends correlated highly with the self-ratings of the individuals in question, thereby offering support for the consensual validity of the scale.

### Other criticisms

Heim (1970) has criticised the construction of both EPI and EPQ because of the limited choice of response available to the respondent (Yes/No). Heim argues that this type of questionnaire cannot do justice to the complex and changeable nature of the human personality. As the above studies relied on the use of a questionnaire, the findings must be interpreted with caution in view of Heim's argument.

Moreover, Kendrick (1981) noted that there have been limited applications of Eysenck's EPQ, and very few clinicians have made use of predictions arising from it when treating individual patients. This may be that because of the nature of mental illness, a more sensitive and humane approach may be required than that generated by the use of a questionnaire.

### New research

In recent years several theorists have extended the framework proposed by Eysenck to include further personality dimensions. Initially this new model became known as 'The Big Five' and included the dimensions of extraversion and neuroticism. The other three were agreeableness, conscientiousness and culture. Further research by Costa and McCrae (1993) confirmed the importance of four of the factors, but proposed replacing the dimension of culture with 'openness to experience'. They have also devised a questionnaire to measure personality known as the NEO-PI five factors inventory (see Figure 3.3).

The big five model of personality was shown to have consensual validity by McCrae and Costa (1987), and so stands as an alternative to Eysenck's EPI and EPQ. In view of this more contemporary measure

| | |
|---|---|
| 1 | Openness to experience |
| 2 | Neuroticism |
| 3 | Conscientiousness |
| 4 | Extraversion |
| 5 | Agreeableness |

*Figure 3.3* **Costa and McCrae's NEO-PI five factors**

of personality the most that can be said of Eysenck's theory of personality is that two of its dimensions, neuroticism and extraversion, have stood the test of time and therefore would appear to be valid measures of human personality. However the most problematic area of Eysenck's theorising is the lack of evidence of a clear biological explanation for the personality scores achieved by individuals, especially concerning the sensitivity of the ANS in introverts. Clinical trials have not found this to be the case. A further difficulty relates to his predictions regarding the conditionability of introverts. As discussed earlier, Eysenck's theory states that because the biological functioning of introverts (including the ANS) is more sensitive than that of extraverts, they should be more easily conditioned. If this were found to be the case then it would stand as powerful evidence that the basis of personality does in fact lie in the biology of the person, as Eysenck believes. However, again this has been found not to be the case.

Write a short summary of the evidence for and against Eysenck's personality theory.

*Progress exercise*

## Allport's trait theory

Gordon Allport was one of the first psychologists to search for a basic core of personality traits that could be used to account for all people. According to Allport (1961) the personality of an individual can be defined as '. . . the dynamic organisation of those psychophysical systems that determine his/her characteristic behaviour and thoughts'. By defining personality in terms of organisation, Allport is emphasising the individualistic nature of personality.

Allport believed that the study of personality should emphasise the uniqueness of humans, and should aim to describe the experiences and psychological structures that determine each individual's way of thinking and behaving. He felt that research into the human personality should focus on individual people, and was not helped by attempting to uncover universal structures, or ways of describing people that can be applied universally. According to Allport the only way of reaching any sort of understanding of people, is to treat them as separate units of experience, which can only be achieved by studying them in a qualitative way, in contrast to the quantitative, score based approach we have seen being employed by Eysenck. This issue will be discussed further in the evaluation section.

## Allport's traits

Allport recognised the existence of personality traits (e.g. generosity), which he saw as permanent mental structures, that make up an individual's personality. He felt that the way an individual behaves and thinks is due to these mental structures, and is fairly consistent over time. So if a person has the generosity trait, then they would be *generous* in most situations.

He viewed language as a starting point for investigating personality, and using a dictionary produced a list of 18,000 adjectives (such as *cheerful* and *lazy*), which could be used to describe a variety of traits (Allport and Odbert 1936). He reduced this list down to approximately 4000 adjectives after omitting those that described either transient states such as *stressed*, or personal evaluations such as *respected*. Allport believed (in line with contemporary trait theorists) that in order to be able to explain human personality, we must first be able to describe it in terms of traits.

The essence of Allport's theory lies in his suggestion that an individual manifests three types of traits, which he described as cardinal traits, central traits or secondary traits.

*Cardinal traits*

Allport considered that some traits have particular influence over an individual's behaviour, and therefore personality. In some cases a single cardinal trait, such as *ambition* or *greed*, might completely dominate the personality. However, according to Allport this is extremely rare and most people are strongly affected by a mixture of cardinal traits.

*Central traits*

Allport thought of these as a cluster of core traits that constitute an individual's particular way of approaching life (e.g. a person's central traits may be *stubborn, truthful, passionate*). These differ from cardinal traits in that they remain fairly constant throughout life, whereas cardinal traits may change according to the situation an individual finds themselves in.

*Secondary traits*

These are the least influential of all traits and represent an individual's preferences, tastes and behaviours which tend to be tailored to specific situations (e.g. at a party a person might be sociable, *loud* and *humorous*, while at a place of work they may be *serious, diligent* and *focused*).

### The uniqueness of traits

Allport argued that the traits which constitute an individual's personality are unique to them in a number of ways. For a start, even if two people are given the same characteristic (i.e. passionate), it may be that for one person it is a cardinal trait (they will behave passionately in certain situations), and for the other person a secondary trait (they will sometimes behave passionately).

Further, the way that one person exhibits a trait may be very different from the way another person exhibits it. As put by Allport, any individual 'is a unique creation of the forces of nature. There was never a person just like him and there never will be again' (Allport 1961).

Lastly, Allport believed that some traits only occur in one person (they are so unique that nobody else has that particular trait). In fact, it seemed to him that there may be as many traits as there are people.

Progress exercise

Explain how Allport devised his personality theory and describe yourself using the three types of traits he puts forward.

## Assessing personality

Allport would assess an individual's personality in a variety of ways. These included open interviews aimed at uncovering the person's ideas and attitudes to life, their short- and long-term goals, and their beliefs. He would also study letters and diaries as well as other written material belonging to the person, in order to build up a detailed account of them. This of course is the case study method favoured by psychologists such as Freud and epitomises the idiographic approach.

## Evaluation of Allport's approach

Allport is often criticised by *nomothetic* theorists, for his rejection of scientific/empirical methods of studying personality. However, his belief in the uniqueness of humans, and his emphasis on the whole person rather than just elements of people (which may or may not be universal), has led to an alternative view of personality.

For Allport the nomothetic approach will always portray human personality in an oversimplified way, one that ignores the idiosyncratic (individual) way that people perform as people. For example, if Sally and Carol are both labelled as aggressive personalities, will their aggression be exactly the same? Probably not, as Allport states: 'common speech is a poor guide to psychological subtleties' (Allport 1961). In other words, if we say that two people are aggressive and leave it at that, we are ignoring the fact that the nature of their aggression may be very different and may be exhibited in different ways, at different times, and for different reasons.

## Comparing Eysenck and Allport

Eysenck argued against this emphasis on uniqueness, although he did recognise that people score unique combinations of levels on trait dimensions. Therefore, he believed that while people are unique, this uniqueness could be described and quantified according to a universal set of principles (i.e. his personality dimensions). For example, one person might be found to be quiet and reserved on the introversion dimension, while another could be pessimistic and anxious on the same dimension. So the dimensions themselves remain the same, but the trait levels differ. Eysenck believed that everyone is more or less extroverted, and all will score somewhere along the extroversion dimension, the only difference being where along the continuum they score.

Allport argued that this idea of individuality is a contradiction in terms. On one hand people are said to be similar in terms of personality and therefore can be grouped together (under one dimension), while on the other they are described as very different from each other, and therefore unique. Allport suggested that only individual traits could capture the uniqueness of people, and because of the vastness and diversity of those traits, they cannot be grouped together under a few dimensions. The idea that different traits represent different levels along a single continuum he found unacceptable.

Holt (1967) suggested that the idiographic approach taken by Allport is really a nomothetic one, but applied to individual cases. He argues that Allport's personality theory uses the same trait characteristics to describe the personality of individuals as do nomothetic researchers such as Eysenck. But instead of grouping them together under a few universal dimensions, Allport emphasises the unique way these traits are expressed in different individuals.

More critical were Kirkby and Radford (1976) who believed that Allport was misguided in mistaking the art of biography (descriptive science), for the scientific study of the individual (empirical science). They argued that while biography gives an insight into the behaviour of individuals, it does not allow a general understanding of human nature.

Review exercise

1 Look at the chart below that shows a similarity and a difference between the two psychologists. Can you think of any more?
2 Discuss the similarity and difference, plus any others you have thought of, using evidence from the chapter.

| | Eysenck | Allport |
|---|---|---|
| **Similarity** | use of descriptive terms (traits or types) | |
| **Difference** | universal dimensions | unique traits |

## Summary

In this chapter we have contrasted the research of two very different researchers, Hans Eysenck and Gordon Allport. Eysenck employed a nomothetic approach to establish the existence of universal dimensions of behaviour, which he called introversion/extraversion, neuroticism/ stability and psychoticism. These ideas have been shown to be valid in a number of ways. For example, the questionnaire developed by Eysenck to support this theory has been shown to be capable of predicting individual behaviour. Eysenck was however less successful in underpinning his ideas with a biological theory of behaviour. Perhaps as a result of this, his ideas have found little clinical application. In contrast to Eysenck, Gordon Allport was an advocate of idiographic research. Allport saw personality as being a result of the organisation of an individual's personality traits. Allport suggested that individuals manifest three types of traits: cardinal traits, central traits or secondary traits, depending on how dominant they are in a person's makeup. Allport viewed the mixture of traits and even the traits themselves as being unique to each individual.

## Further reading

Eysenck, H.J. (1977) *Psychology is about people*, London: Pelican Books. Gives a firsthand account of Eysenck's ideas about personality.

Eysenck, M. (1997) *Simply Psychology*, Hove: Psychology Press. An easy-to-read yet detailed explanation of Eysenck's and Allport's theories.

Kline, P. (1983) *Personality – measurement and theory*, London: Hutchinson. Concise but clear explanation of theories and a useful explanation of measurements used.

Rust, J. and Golombok, S. (1992) *Modern Psychometrics, The Science of Psychological Assessment*, London and New York: Routledge. An in-depth discussion of psychometrics and its use in social psychology.

# 4

# Psychoanalytic theory

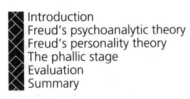

Introduction
Freud's psychoanalytic theory
Freud's personality theory
The phallic stage
Evaluation
Summary

## Introduction

All psychoanalytic approaches to the study of personality (sometimes referred to as psychodynamic approaches) are derived from the work of Sigmund Freud. These include the work of theorists such as Erik Erikson (whom we shall discuss later in this chapter), Carl Jung, Adolf Adler, Melanie Klein and Anna Freud. Their work is based on the idea that our behaviour (and therefore our personality) is shaped and controlled by dynamic driving inner forces. These forces consist of our instincts, needs, desires and morals. They are shaped by our past experiences, and are in a state of continual conflict with each other.

It used to be popularly assumed that human behaviour is determined by rational thoughts that the individual is consciously aware of. For example, if we behave aggressively we should be aware of the reasons why we are behaving in that way, and be able to explain them. Or, if we feel sad and spend our time moping around the house, there would be a logical reason behind it. However Freud opposed this belief, claiming that the reasons for our behaviour are seldom consciously available to us, and are often irrational. We may feel angry or sad and have no explanation for why we feel this way. Freud also believed that the forces of our unconscious mind finds modes of expression in our patterns of behaviour and attitudes for which we have no rational explanation. To the psychoanalyst this reveals evidence of unresolved life experiences, which at the time they occurred we may have found traumatic, and so repressed them. These beliefs laid the foundations for the subsequent development of psychoanalytic theories.

## Freud's psychoanalytic theory

Sigmund Freud (1856–1939) trained as a doctor in Vienna where he specialised in neurological disorders (disorders of the nervous system). He worked under the direction of physiologist Ernst Wilhelm von Brucke. In 1874, Brucke proposed that the human organism is a dynamic system that can be explained with the same laws that apply to physics and chemistry. In other words the behaviour of humans could be explained by predetermined laws, a concept we describe as **determinism**. This was to have a profound influence on Freud's thoughts and, later, the development of his personality theory.

A further influence on Freud's thoughts came from the famous German physicist Helmholtz, who had formulated a law concerning the conservation of energy. He stated that energy (like mass) cannot be *destroyed*, but only *transformed*. Freud applied these two principles to his explanation of personality. He stated that personality is a dynamic system that works to laws and principles. The energy produced by this system, which may be in the form of aggression or desire etc., cannot just disappear, but must find a release through some action of the person. For example, the energy could be released in a positive way through taking up a sport.

So, staying with the idea that personality is dynamic and produces energy, Freud began to search for a psychological explanation of personality. The answer became clearer to Freud while treating patients with neurological problems. He began to suspect that many symptoms, such as hysteria, had no underlying physical basis, even though they were experienced by the patient as if they had. He needed to find a treatment for his patients that took into account the lack of a physical explanation, and a psychological theory to explain it all.

A final influence on Freud came from the French neurologist Charcot, who was investigating the use of hypnosis with patients suffering from hysteria (a name given to any illness with no physical explanation). Freud began working with him, and initially felt that this treatment was the answer. However, he later discovered that hypnosis was not enough to cure his patients, many of whom began to suffer from heightened symptoms after treatment. This led him to develop new types of treatment such as the technique of **free association**, whereby the patient is encouraged to say the first word that comes into his or her head, following a word given by the therapist. Freud believed that this method tapped into the unconscious mind of the patient without the use of hypnosis. The use of free association proved to be highly successful and has continued to be one of the core treatments offered by psychoanalysts today.

### The conscious, preconscious and unconscious mind

Freud's understanding of personality grew from all of the influences mentioned above, but before we go on to discuss his actual theory of personality, it is important to note how he saw the individual mind.

Freud defined the **conscious** mind as that which we are aware of every day. For example, how we feel, what we perceive and think about, our current memories and our fantasies. Working alongside the conscious mind is what Freud called the **preconscious**, which consists of any thoughts that we can easily make conscious. For example, in the preconscious could reside memories of past events, recollections of how things work, or recognition of people or places etc. However, according to Freud, these two levels of the human mind (the conscious and the preconscious) are extremely small in comparison with the unconscious.

The **unconscious** is believed to take up a huge part of our psyche, and contains all the things that are not easily available to awareness. This would include things like drives and instincts, for example the drive to obtain food or the instinctual need for sex. Also contained in the unconscious would be memories and emotions that are too painful for us to make conscious. These could be traumatic events that we have experienced personally, or perhaps disturbing scenes we may have witnessed. The memories of such occurrences would cause us distress and so to protect our psyche (our minds) from such trauma, according to Freud we bury these memories deep in our unconscious mind. We no longer remember the event itself, even though it is still part of our memory: we have made it inaccessible to our conscious mind. In the short term this is a good way of protecting ourselves, but in the long run we create all sorts of problems for ourselves (we will come back to this later in the chapter when we discuss defence mechanisms).

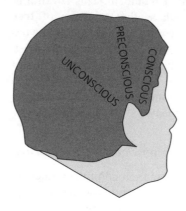

*Figure 4.1* **Symbolic representation of conscious/preconscious/ unconscious mind**

## Freud's personality theory

So far we have looked at the human mind and how Freud believed it worked, but what about his personality theory? Well, it actually consists of three theories. The first focuses on how we conduct ourselves throughout our lives and concerns three major parts, the **id**, **ego** and **superego**. The second theory focuses on the idea of **defence mechanisms** that Freud believed we use to stop ourselves feeling too much anxiety or guilt. The third theory is what Freud called the **psychosexual stages** and maps our sexual development from infancy, through childhood and into adulthood.

Answer the following questions:

1 How does the preconscious differ from the unconscious? Give examples to illustrate the difference.
2 Name the three parts of Freud's personality theory.

Progress exercise

### The id, ego and superego

According to Freudian theory a very important part of the human organism is the nervous system (this is where Freud makes the link with biology), which is highly sensitive to the needs of the organism. In a human infant the nervous system is linked to what Freud calls the id which works to fulfil the needs of the infant. The id translates the infant's needs into **instincts** or **drives** (or wishes as Freud liked to call them). This process, from need to drive, is known as the **primary process** (Freud 1976).

The id works on the basis of the **pleasure principle**, which is to seek out pleasure and avoid pain. In fulfilling the needs of the infant the id can bring about satisfaction, and therefore pleasure. A further point to note is that the id demands immediate fulfilment of needs. An example of this in action is a screaming infant that wants to be fed. The infant has no concept of social restrictions or that it may have to wait a while, it wants to be fed immediately.

The ego comes about as the infant begins to adapt to the outside world. This happens when the conscious part of the mind, which is linked to reality through the senses, begins to search for ways of satisfying the needs of the id, this is known as the **secondary process**. Unlike the id, the ego operates on the **reality principle**. This means that although it will attempt to satisfy the needs of the infant, it will only do so realistically. For example, the fulfilment of the need for food would be postponed until the appropriate time and place. The ego will always take into account social restrictions and practical realities. In this way the ego can be thought of as the manager of the personality as it attempts to balance the needs/desires of the id and the realities of the world outside.

The third part of Freud's personality theory concerns the superego, which can be thought of as the individual's internal moral code. This part of the personality does not emerge until the child is approximately 4–6 years old. The superego is formed from the moral sanctions and inhibitions that have been internalised by the child due to the intervention of the ego operating through the reality principle in its attempt to satisfy the needs of the id.

There are two aspects to the superego: one is the **conscience** and the other the **ego ideal**.

*Conscience*

This part of the superego is concerned with what is wrong or bad. It internalises punishments and warnings in order to censor immoral impulses from the id and so avoid punishment.

*Ego ideal*

Here the concern is focused on what is right and good. The ego ideal represents the type of behaviour that will be rewarded, that is seen as positive and that should be encouraged.

Together the conscience and ego ideal communicate their needs to the ego with feelings like shame and guilt in terms of the conscience, or pride and self-respect in terms of the ego ideal. And in this way help shape the behaviour of the individual.

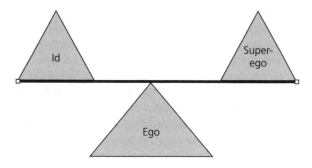

*Figure 4.2* **Symbolic representation of id/ego/superego**

Freud assumed that the three main components of the personality, the id, the ego and the superego, are in constant conflict with each other. The id continues to demand instant fulfilment of needs and desires, while the superego constantly thwarts these needs by setting high (sometimes unreasonably high) moral standards. The ego has the job of balancing the demands of these two opposing forces along with the external demands of society. Any unresolved conflict caused by this dynamic flux results in anxiety for the individual, which can manifest itself in dreams or as neurotic behaviour. In order to explain how we cope with this anxiety Freud put forward a further theory concerning defence mechanisms.

### Defence mechanisms

As we have said, the ego has the job of balancing the needs and desires of the id and the superego. At times this can be a difficult and anxiety-provoking job, as the ego has to work extremely hard to keep everything under control or else risk being overwhelmed by it all. When this becomes too difficult the ego must protect itself from too much anxiety, and does so by blocking or distorting the flood of impulses from the id and superego and turning them into something more acceptable. Freud called these **ego defence mechanisms** and they are brought about in three ways:

- *Moral conflict*: the ego versus the superego. For example the impulse to do something that the superego would find morally wrong, e.g. telling lies, commiting a crime,
- *Neurotic conflict*: the ego versus the id. Here the ego is in fear of being overwhelmed by strong id impulses and may lose control. An example would be losing your temper or your rationality.
- *Realistic conflict*: the ego versus reality. For example when the person is faced with a situation that provokes feelings of fear, e.g. threats of violence, abuse etc.

When one of the above reactions is experienced by the ego it will react by employing a defence mechanism. There are many different strategies or mechanisms the ego can employ and although Freud put forward quite a few, others have been discovered and added to the list by his daughter Anna Freud. The following are the most commonly cited:

*Repression*

According to Freud this is the most basic defence mechanism and is employed most often. Labelled 'motivated forgetting' by Anna Freud, repression means that the ego forces the impulse or memory out of conscious awareness and into the unconscious so the individual is unable to recall the threatening situation, person or event. As stated by Anna Freud (1936): 'The essence of repression lies simply in the function of rejecting and keeping something out of consciousness'.

*Denial*

This is where the ego blocks from conscious awareness external events that are too painful or too difficult to handle. An example may be that the individual suddenly discovers a physical abnormality but doesn't do anything about it, refusing to believe they may require medical attention. They are in denial and therefore refuse to accept reality.

*Isolation*

This defence mechanism is sometimes called intellectualisation and means that in certain situations or when recalling particular memories, a person will show no emotion or feeling. They may recall painful events without recalling the emotion that they felt at the time. An example may be that a person recalls how they were abused as a child, but acts as if it meant nothing to them.

*Projection*

This is when the ego cannot cope with unacceptable id desires and so turns them into the desires of other people. An example could be of a person who often feels angry and aggressive towards others, but continually accuses others of being aggressive themselves. Or a person may feel sexually attracted to the husband or wife of a friend, and, unable to accept these feelings, becomes increasingly worried about the faithfulness of their own partner. To use the defence mechanism of projection is to put onto others feelings of your own which you'd rather not acknowledge.

*Reaction formation*

Anna Freud called this 'believing the opposite', and it occurs when the ego changes an unacceptable impulse into its opposite. For example, a child feels anger towards its parent, but finding this feeling unacceptable becomes overly concerned for the parent's welfare. Or a mother feels irritation and anger towards her newborn infant but cannot accept that she could feel this way and so reacts by becoming obsessed with being a good parent.

This is where a person behaves in a way that in the past may have brought about relief from an anxiety-provoking situation. An example may be of an older child reverting to sucking his or her thumb when another child is born into the family. Or an adult may throw a tantrum if things aren't going the way he or she wants them to.

These are a few examples of the most common defence mechanisms that Freud and others, such as Anna Freud, have discussed.

## The psychosexual stages

The final part of Freud's personality theory concerns the sexual energy or libido of the individual as they pass through various stages in their life. Freud believed that sexual energy was the most important motivating force throughout people's lives (Freud 1977). However sexual energy doesn't just mean intercourse, but refers to all pleasurable sensations felt with our bodies. This could mean kissing, stroking, touching or even just holding someone, as well as the more obvious sexual encounters.

Freud noted that at different times in our lives we gain greatest pleasure from different parts of our bodies. Later theorists called these areas erogenous zones. From this observation Freud proposed five stages of psychosexual development, so called because of the link between sexuality and the mind. He believed that for young infants the focus of sexual pleasure (and therefore the infant's erogenous zone) is the mouth. Initially this pleasure is through sucking, especially at the breast. As the infant grows older the erogenous zone expands to include the anal area where the child derives most pleasure from the power to hold onto or let go of, the faeces. At approximately 3 years old the child's erogenous zone changes again, this time the focus moving to the genitals. Pleasure is felt from rubbing or stroking this area. Freud named this the phallic stage, during which he believed that the child goes through what he calls the Oedipal complex. This is when the child is caught up in an emotional/sexual struggle with its mother and father, which the child must resolve if it is to successfully establish its own sexual identity and avoid neurosis as an adult. This is one of the most controversial of Freud's ideas, and we will discuss both the theory itself and an evaluation of it in detail later in this chapter. The phallic stage continues until the child is about 6 years old when they enter what Freud calls the latency period, in which sexual pleasures are forgotten for a while. Lastly, from puberty onwards the final stage, called the genital stage, is reached, where sexual pleasure is gained from adult sexual encounters.

Each psychosexual stage brings with it psychological challenges that the child must overcome. Freud believed that if a child fails to negotiate any stage of psychosexual development successfully then he or she will become **fixated** at that particular stage. When this happens the child (and eventually the adult) will retain some of the characteristics of that stage. For example, a child fixated at the oral stage will continue to derive pleasure through the mouth, perhaps by sucking the thumb throughout childhood. As an adult that same child may take up smoking or some other habit that entails putting something into the mouth. According to Freud, if the fixation is severe, or if the child has been subjected to any kind of sexual abuse, this may result in neurosis as an adult. In fact, Freud stated that all neurosis has its basis in childhood, and is linked to any sexual activity that is experienced as negative by the child, whether their involvement is passive or active (Freud 1977).

The following is a brief explanation of each stage of psychosexual development:

*Oral Stage (birth to 1 year)*

The personality is dominated by the id, and sexual energy is centred on the mouth. Sucking and biting bring pleasure. The task associated with this stage is weaning which must be accomplished without too much anxiety if the child is to negotiate the stage successfully and avoid fixation.

*Anal stage (2–3 years)*

Here the focus of sexual energy is on the anal region and consists of holding onto and letting go of the faeces. Fixation occurs if potty training causes anxiety, and manifests itself in the adult personality as obsessiveness, meanness and often a preoccupation with cleanliness.

*Phallic stage (4–6 years)*

The genitals are the focus of sexual energy, and successful negotiation of the Oedipal complex leads to identification with the same sex parent and the adoption of the moral standards and attitudes of that parent which, along with the norms of society, form the child's superego. According to Freud, fixation at this stage leads to adult neurosis.

*Latency period (6 – puberty)*

This is when sexual energy lies dormant and learning takes over. The development of the ego in terms of the child's intellect, as well as social skills, becomes the main focus.

*Genital stage (puberty)*

Sexual energy emerges once more and true adult sexuality begins to develop with the focus on sexual intercourse. This final stage represents the accumulation of all the other stages, which if negotiated successfully, leads to a well-balanced and healthy sexual adult.

## The phallic stage

Of all the stages proposed by Freud the most important in terms of personality development is the phallic stage, which the child enters at around 4 years of age. If this stage is successfully negotiated then the child identifies with their gender role and acquires their superego. Freud named the conflict that epitomises this stage the Oedipal complex, from the ancient Greek god Oedipus who inadvertently slept with his mother and killed his father. This may give you some idea of the challenge that the child must negotiate successfully in order to fulfil the requirements of this particular stage (see Box 4.1 for a detailed explanation of the Oedipal complex).

Some theorists rightly feel that Freud ought to have provided a separate explanation for the resolution of the Oedipal complex in females. However, Freud's knowledge of some aspects of female sexuality, namely female masturbation, was by his own admission, regretfully lacking. Therefore, although he did discuss female sexuality (Freud 1933), and provide a description of the female's resolution of her own Oedipal complex, he was unable to analyse it in as much detail as he was the male complex. There has been some reference to the female complex as the Electra complex (e.g. Jung 1913) but Freud himself never used this term.

Progress exercise

Without looking back at the previous descriptions, see if you can list Freud's psychosexual stages, giving a brief description of each stage, include the approximate ages at which each stage occurs.

---

### *Box 4.1* **The Oedipal complex**

The conflict facing the child in the phallic stage of psychosexual development centres on the penis. For boys, Freud believed that initially the child desired his mother above all else, but was afraid of his father whom he saw as a rival for his mother's love. At about the same time the boy also realises that whereas he has a penis, his mother, and in fact all females, do not. The young boy has no idea why females should not have a penis and can only assume that it must have been removed. The boy links this discovery with his father whom he feels may have been the one to remove the female's penis and therefore has the power to castrate him. This is what Freud calls **castration fear** and causes the boy to displace his sexual preferences from his mother to other girls, while at the same time identifying himself with the aggressor (his father) in an attempt to become more like him, and eventually to take on his role as a male.

For girls the Oedipal complex takes place in a similar way, except that when the girl becomes aware of her lack of a penis she feels what Freud calls **penis envy**. She seeks to rectify this by forging a strong attachment to her father (who does have a penis), in order to gain a substitute for her lack of penis, such as a baby. This is an unacceptable state of affairs and so eventually the girl displaces her affection for her father to other boys and identifies with her mother, thereby internalising her role as a female in society.

## Evaluation

There have been a number of objections to Freud's theory of personality, but the two commonest criticisms are:

1 the lack of **empirical evidence** to support his many claims about the essence of who we are and what we are about;
2 the fact that Freud's theories cannot predict behaviour but only explain it. For example, using Freud's defence mechanism of regression may explain why an older child reverts to sucking their thumb, but would be unable to predict that this would happen.

The following discussion looks at specific areas of Freudian theory to highlight both strengths and weaknesses.

### The unconscious mind

The idea that we repress experiences that we find traumatic and that this then leads us to manifest all sorts of personality disorders (from phobias to psychosis) has caused a great deal of debate. Most theorists today believe that the motivations and problems attributed to the unconscious are much fewer than Freud postulated. In fact, many theorists see no benefit in even considering the concept of the unconscious. As pointed out by Popper (1959), Freud's theory of the unconscious mind (including id impulses, defence mechanisms etc.) not only cannot be supported, but also cannot be refuted, which according to Popper is a serious violation of the scientific method. However, Kline (1989) argues that although parts of Freud's theory (such as the unconscious mind) cannot be proven or disproven, there are other aspects of the theory that can. For example, most of the psychosexual stages of development are based on observable behaviours. Kline believes where possible this testing should be carried out in a scientific and objective manner, endorsing Freud's theories with some credibility, and encouraging others to continue investigating Freudian concepts.

### The Oedipal complex

One of the most controversial aspects of Freud's theories is the idea that infants and young children have sexual experiences and feel sexual pleasure. Although, as we said earlier, this does not refer to adult sexual pleasure (e.g. sexual intercourse), but to any form of touching, stroking or simply holding that brings pleasure to the child. According to Freud, the Oedipal complex is the most important stage in the child's psychosexual development and influence on their adult personality, but the evidence put forward that it even exists is very thin on the ground. For example, as noted by Stevens (1995), Freud used his own retrospective thinking, along with case studies of adult patients suffering from neurosis, and just one case study involving a child, to come up with a whole theory about how children develop sexually. Also the one case study that does involve a child – Little Hans (Freud 1922) (described below) – does not in itself constitute objective evidence of the theory of psychosexual development.

### Analysis of a phobia in a 5-year-old boy

This case study of a young boy called Hans is the main piece of evidence Freud uses to illustrate his theory of psychosexual stages and the Oedipal complex. Hans was the child of parents who were great believers in Freud's theories, and as such applied these theories to their son's behaviour. The boy's father analysed Hans' behaviour from a Freudian perspective and communicated this analysis to Freud in the form of letters. Freud only ever met Hans on a couple of occasions and his interpretation of Hans' behaviour was entirely based on the information supplied to him by the boy's father.

The following is some of the evidence Hans' father sent to Freud concerning Hans' behaviour:

At approximately 3 years old Hans suddenly began to have anxiety attacks. During one of these attacks Hans told his father that he wanted to be ill in order to stay with his mother and 'coax' (cuddle) with her. He also displayed a fear of horses, in particular a white horse with a black mouth and blinkers.

Hans began to show a 'peculiarly lively interest in his widdler (penis)', an organ which Hans believed all animate objects possessed. This interest led to his mother's threatening to 'cut off his widdler' if he didn't stop playing with it, when Hans was 3½ years old.

The birth of his sister led to signs of jealousy from Hans, such as his wish that she would drown in the bath.

Hans began to have lots of different fantasies. One example concerns two giraffes. One was small and crumpled while the other was big. In the fantasy Hans held the small, crumpled giraffe in his hand while the big one called out. He then sat on the small one and the big one went away. This fantasy was thought by Freud to relate to Hans' parents: the small giraffe being his mother and the big one his father.

Freud interpreted all of this 'evidence' as part of Hans' psychosexual development and negotiation of the Oedipal complex. The need to be with his mother illustrated the beginning of Hans' Oedipal complex. His fear of horses was thought to represent Hans' fear that his father might castrate him (the black mouth of the horse was his father's moustache and the blinkers his father's glasses). The death wish towards his sister again represented the Oedipal need to have his mother to himself. The various fantasies were interpreted as symbolic of Hans' repressed desires concerning his sexual development. Particularly the desire to get rid of his father, so that he may have his mother to himself.

Typical criticisms of the case study of Little Hans include:

1  Freud had already devised his theory concerning the Oedipal complex in his writings, *Three Essays on the Theory of Sexuality* (1905), and simply interpreted the behaviour of Hans to fit the theory. This is an example of the explanatory rather than the predictive power of the theory.
2  Freud met Hans on only a few occasions; most of the interviewing of Hans was conducted by the little boy's father, an avid follower and believer of Freudian theory. This again invalidates the data as not only can it be assumed that the father will be biased in his accounts of Hans' behaviour, but also he could easily influence his son's behaviour in a way that fits the theory.
3  Freud's interpretation of Hans' behaviour is only one of a number of logical explanations that could account for it. The most notable alternative explanations were later put forward by two eminent psychoanalysts, Erich Fromm and John Bowlby.

### Erich Fromm's explanation

Fromm (1970) points out that the era in which Freud lived had an impact on his views and also his theories. Although radically against bourgeois society and all it stood for, especially in terms of how children were treated (namely with strict discipline and restrictive narrow views), Freud didn't have the strength of his convictions. He changed his original 'seduction theory' which positioned children as innocent victims of incest, and replaced it with the Oedipal complex that saw children not as victims but as perpetrators of their own sexuality. This theory was much more likely to be accepted by society at that time, as it fit in with current thinking rather than radically opposing it. So, with the parents absolved of their incestuous fantasies, any occurrences that pointed towards that very thing were reinterpreted as the child's desires and fantasies. Fromm points out that Hans' mother appeared to have many fantasies concerning her small son, which were apparent in her need to have him in bed with her and accompany her to the toilet. Also during the therapy of little Hans the mother threatened to 'cut off his widdler' if he didn't stop messing with it. Fromm believes that it was his mother that Little Hans was afraid of due to her threats and fantasies and not the father at all. In fact, as Fromm notes, Hans' relationship with his father was warm and caring.

### John Bowlby's explanation

Bowlby (1973), in agreement with Fromm, states that Hans' anxieties do indeed stem from his mother. However, Bowlby believes it was the mother's threats to leave the family (which she would often use as a threat to discipline Hans) that provoked the most anxiety. Bowlby links this to his own attachment theory, arguing that Hans is suffering from separation anxiety, rather than anxieties caused by Oedipal desires as Freud stated.

Both of these alternative explanations of Hans' anxieties undermine the Oedipal theory, and therefore cast doubt on the whole theory of psychosexual development.

---

Review exercise

Describe the case of Little Hans, explaining Freud's interpretation of this case study, as well as John Bowlby's and Erich Fromm's.

### Evaluation of defence mechanisms

There has been lots of research into defence mechanisms as they are seen as a part of Freud's theory for which it may be possible to find evidence. Wilkinson and Cargill (1955) carried out a study whereby they related various fictional stories to an experimental group. They found that those stories with an Oedipal theme (therefore causing some anxiety) were less well remembered than those without. This may provide evidence for the defence mechanism of repression. Levinger and Clark (1961) carried out a similar study using words instead of stories. They related lists of words to participants who were asked to respond to each word by coming up with an associated word. They found that when asked to recall their own response words, participants were less likely to remember those words with an emotional association than those that were neutral. This was taken to indicate that the emotional words were being repressed due to their anxiety-provoking status. However, although both of these studies appear to provide evidence for the defence mechanism of repression, they lack any real emotion or real anxiety. According to Freud the individual would have to experience anxiety in a very traumatic way before the ego would employ the defence mechanism of repression, making the above studies invalid.

## Summary

In this chapter we have described the various influences that led Freud to develop his theory of personality. We have discussed his ideas concerning the mind and consciousness, along with his belief that the human organism is a dynamic force shaped by inner needs and instincts. We have described in detail Freud's theory of personality, both defining and explaining the id, ego and superego. We have also discussed Freud's theory of psychosexual stages, and have focused particularly on the phallic stage and the resolution of the Oedipal complex. According to Freud this resolution is crucial if we are to attain psychosexual health as adults. We have also looked at Freud's theory of defence mechanisms. Finally we have evaluated Freud's theoretical ideas, his theory of personality and defence mechanisms. We have also discussed other theorists' points of view, namely John Bowlby and Eric Fromm, and have seen how they oppose some of Freud's beliefs.

## Further reading

Gross, R.D. (1998) *Key Studies in Psychology* (second edition), London: Hodder and Stoughton. This book gives a detailed account of the Hans study.

Richards, A. (ed.) (1979) *On Sexuality: Three essays on the theory of sexuality and other works*, The Penguin Freud Library 7, Harmondsworth: Penguin. Gives a firsthand account of Freud's ideas and beliefs concerning sexuality, and further discussion of female sexual development.

# Social learning
# approaches

## Introduction

The social learning approach to personality is very different from the approaches we have covered so far. Theorists such as Eysenck and Allport are interested in how people behave in terms of personality traits (either universal or unique descriptions), while psychoanalytic theorists focus on the unconscious instincts and motivations that shape our personalities. Both of these approaches emphasise the individual as the site of enquiry, therefore, both are ignoring the effect of society on the individual.

Social learning theorists, on the other hand, are concerned with the *consequences* of our behaviour that act to shape the people we eventually become. These consequences are drawn from the society in which we live. We learn to behave in particular ways at specific times and places through our life experience. We observe how others behave (either directly or on the TV or through reading about them in books) and we see how certain behaviours bring rewards or punishments. These observations interact with our cognitive processes (our beliefs, perceptions and memories) and cause us to behave in particular ways. These are the fundamental beliefs of social learning theory of whom the founder is Albert Bandura.

## Bandura's social learning theory

Albert Bandura, a psychologist and lecturer at Stanford University, California, began his career under the influence of **behaviourism** during the course of his studies as a psychology student in the 1960s. A strong supporter of the work of B. F. Skinner (the most influential behaviourist), Bandura initially agreed with Skinner that all behaviour is caused/shaped by external stimuli in the form of reward and punishment, and any changes in behaviour can only be accounted for by changes in the external environment.

The emphasis behaviourists placed on experimental methods, with a focus on observable variables that could be manipulated and measured, led to an easy acceptance of the theory. It provided evidence for the scientific and therefore objective basis of psychology, which many researchers were hoping to achieve. Behaviour could be tested, and the ensuing data could be used to predict and possibly control behaviour.

Bandura, although a supporter of Skinner's theory, believed his explanations were too simplistic and there must be more to understanding human personality than as just a response to the environment. During this time Bandura was conducting research into aggression in adolescents, and from his observations noted that the effect of the environment was far more complex than Skinner's behaviourist theory allowed. While he agreed that the environment caused behaviour, he saw that behaviour also had an effect on the environment. In other words the situation we are in may cause us to behave in a certain way, but the way we behave will have a further effect on the situation we are in. Bandura called this concept **reciprocal determinism**. He later developed the idea of reciprocal determinism to include three factors: an individual's behaviour, the environment, and psychological factors. He believed that all three interact with each other to produce an individual's personality. This added a cognitive component to the theory and signified Bandura's move away from behaviourism and towards **cognitivism**.

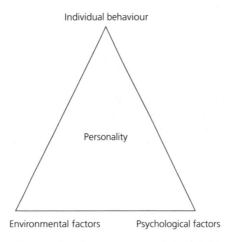

Individual behaviour

Personality

Environmental factors          Psychological factors

*Figure 5.1* **Three factors that interact to create an individual's personality**

1   What is meant by the term cognitivism?

2   Explain what Bandura meant by reciprocal determinism.

Progress exercise

Bandura's ideas collectively became known as **social learning theory**, and although it includes the three components mentioned earlier (behaviour, environment and psychological factors), the theory centres mainly on the cognitive component of human personality. This cognitive component meant that Bandura could introduce the idea that people use imagery and language in order to make sense of their world. This led to the two most important factors in social learning theory: observational learning and self-regulation.

## Observational learning

Sometimes called 'modelling', observational learning is learning through observing the consequences of other peoples' behaviour. For example, a child may observe her older brother taking the dirty dinner plates out into the kitchen to be washed. The important point to note is the consequence of the behaviour, so that if the child witnesses her brother being praised for his action then this sets up an expectation that taking the dishes into the kitchen is a good thing to do and the child learns the behaviour. If however the boy is scolded because he accidently drops and breaks a dish then the consequences of his behaviour are negative and the expectation becomes fear of a scolding. Therefore the observer learns to avoid that type of behaviour.

---

### Box 5.1 The bobo doll studies

These studies were conducted in order to investigate if children would imitate the behaviours they observed in adults. Various studies were conducted such as the following:

Three groups of nursery school children were chosen to watch a film of an adult model behaving aggressively towards a large plastic doll (known as a bobo doll). Each group was exposed to an adult model attacking the bobo doll in a stylised fashion. For example the model would punch the bobo while saying things like 'sockeroo', and 'he sure is a tough fella', and hit the bobo with a mallet, sit on it and throw it across the floor. Although all three groups were exposed to the same behaviour, they each observed a different outcome to that behaviour. One group saw the adult model being given sweets, another group saw the adult told off and smacked, while the third group didn't see either reward or punishment. After watching this performance the children were placed in a room with a bobo doll and other toys and observed to see how they would behave. The children who had seen the adult model rewarded and those who hadn't seen any outcome were equally aggressive towards the bobo doll, whereas the group that had seen the adult model punished were less aggressive. Overall Bandura concluded that children learn through observation in two ways: 1) They learn new ways of behaving (in this case being aggressive). 2) If exposed to aggressive behaviour that is either rewarded or ignored they become generally more aggressive.

---

Review exercise

See if you can draw a cartoon strip to illustrate Bandura's bobo doll study (see Box 5.1).

Bandura (1961, 1963, 1965) conducted a set of famous studies known as the bobo doll studies, to investigate observational learning (see Box 5.1). These studies consisted of exposing groups of children to an adult (**social model**) acting aggressively towards a bobo doll (a large inflatable doll), and then observing the children at play to see if they would imitate the behaviour of the adult they had witnessed. The findings were conclusive, the children did imitate the behaviour of the adult to a significant degree in all of the trials. From these studies, Bandura was able to expand his ideas concerning observational learning, to include all of the factors that can play a part in a person learning a behaviour. They are as follows:

1 *Attention*: in order to learn effectively the observer must be paying attention to the behaviour in question. Distractions include: feeling tired, ill, nervous or under the effect of drugs or drink, or if something else is holding the individual's attention. Also the appearance of the model has an effect on attention. If the model is bright and colourful, appears competent, is attractive or familiar, then the observers pay more attention and so learns the behaviour.

2 *Retention*: the observer must be able to remember what they have seen in order to be able to reproduce it. Imagery and language play a big part here, as what we have observed must be stored in the memory. This occurs either as a mental image, or as a verbal description.

3 *Reproduction*: the observer must also have the ability to reproduce the behaviour they have observed. For example, just because you sit and watch an Oscar-winning performance by a famous film star doesn't mean you can reproduce that behaviour yourself. Although, if you are an actor, then observing the performance could improve

your own acting skills. Another factor in reproduction is practise: the more we practise a behaviour, the more competent we become. Also, if we imagine ourselves performing a behaviour this also improves it.

4 *Motivation*: the main factor in learning from observation. Without motivation we have no chance of ever learning the behaviour. Bandura put forward a number of ways we become motivated to learn behaviour (note the link back to Skinner's ideas concerning learning):

i past reinforcement – learning from rewards (true behaviourism);
ii promised reinforcement – learning from incentives;
iii vicarious reinforcement – seeing others rewarded.

There are also motivators that encourage us not to repeat certain behaviours:

i past punishment;
ii promised punishment;
iii vicarious punishment.

**Progress exercise**

1 List the four factors that influence an individual learning a behaviour, and explain how they work.
2 Think of an example where you have learned a particular behaviour using one of Bandura's factors. For example, you may have learned a dance step from watching *Top of the Pops*, because you were able to *reproduce* it while you watched.

Bandura, like Skinner, believes that, in terms of learning, being punished does not work as well as being rewarded, and warns that it may lead to the opposite effect whereby the person deliberately avoids the said/hoped-for behaviour and initiates the inappropriate behaviour. This is because punishment only teaches us what is the wrong behaviour, and not how to behave appropriately. It also sets up a negative relationship between the person doing the punishing, and the person being punished. This could cause the wrongdoer to feel antagonistic towards the punisher.

## Self-regulation

This refers to how we control our own behaviour, and along with observational learning is an important part of Bandura's theory in terms of personality development. Self-regulation occurs in various ways, but ultimately leads us to monitor and control our own responses to the world in which we live. Self-observation and judgement are two ways in which this happens. We constantly look at ourselves and our behaviour and judge whether our performance is up to scratch by comparing ourselves with various other standards. These would include, for example, comparing our behaviour with that of other people, with traditional cultural standards (those learned from others, e.g. politeness) and of course with our own arbitrary standards (those we create ourselves, e.g. a promise to carry out charity work). We respond to these self-observations by rewarding or punishing ourselves, according to how well we feel we are doing. For example, if we feel we are doing well in comparison to others then we may reward ourselves with a new outfit, or a night out. If on the other hand we feel we are doing badly, then we may punish ourselves by working when we could be having fun. Other ways in which we are rewarded or punished are through feelings of pride or shame brought about by our actions. These acts of self-regulation also have an effect on our self-esteem.

## Self-esteem

The concept of **self-esteem** relates to the overall view (self-image) we have of ourselves and whether that view makes us feel happy and confident or insecure and inadequate. For example, if we feel that we cope well in a crisis, are reliable and trustworthy, and talented in terms of our work, then the chances are that our self-esteem will be high. If on the other hand we see ourselves as unable to cope with the problems we face, irresponsible and lacking in ability, then it's likely that our self-esteem will be low. So, if the ways we view ourselves are positive and encouraging then our self-esteem should be high, but if we are constantly putting ourselves down and feeling inadequate then obviously our self-esteem suffers.

Self-regulation is also linked to self-esteem, as the way in which we judge our own behaviour will culminate in high or low self-esteem.

As we go through our lives our self-esteem is constantly changing. If we are continually punishing ourselves because we feel we are never able to meet our own standards, then our self-esteem will remain low. For example, we may do badly in an exam, or fail to complete a work project, or we may want to participate in some charity work but never find the time. If on the other hand we meet the standards we set for ourselves, and so often give ourselves praise and rewards, then our self-esteem is likely to be high.

### Self-punishment

As already noted, Bandura believes (as did Skinner) that punishment often has a negative effect on behaviour and may even lead to unwanted behaviours being reinforced. Self-punishment has a similar effect. Bandura has put forward three likely consequences of too much self-punishment:

1 **escapism**: this could be in the form of drink, drugs or other addictions such as TV, gambling etc.;
2 **inactivity**: feeling apathetic, bored, lack of direction, depression;
3 **compensation**: making up for perceived failure by a pretence of superiority which may lead to **delusions of grandeur**.

These consequences can in themselves cause all sorts of problems for the individual: as well as low self-esteem the person may evolve an unhealthy personality that continually adopts a negative attitude towards themselves. Bandura recommended that the person takes three steps towards changing their unhealthy self-image. First they must observe themselves in a fair and accurate way, focusing on positive as well as negative elements of their personality. Second they should make sure their standards aren't so high that they are bound to fail. And last they should always use self-reward rather than self-punishment. Any person who punishes themselves to an extreme may need professional help, in order to prevent further negative behaviours and psychological deterioration.

### Self-efficacy

The final concept that formed part of Bandura's explanation of personality is that of **self-efficacy**, which can be defined as how successful we believe we will be in a given situation. According to Bandura (1982), whether we make changes and adapt to our environment (or not) depends to a large extent on our level of self-efficacy. For example, if we have behaved in a particular way in the past and achieved success (i.e. were rewarded) then our self-efficacy will be high. The chances of us reproducing that behaviour when faced with a similar situation is also high, as we believe (having learnt from experience) that our behaviour will lead to a successful outcome. If on the other hand we find ourselves in a situation that we have experienced in the past as one we cannot successfully negotiate, then our self-efficacy will be low and we may become apathetic and withdraw from trying to succeed.

The concept of self-efficacy is linked with self-esteem, and whether we have an optimistic or a pessimistic view of life. If our self-efficacy is high then the other self-beliefs tend to follow suit. For example, if we feel we can successfully pass an exam then our self-efficacy is high, our self-esteem is also high as we see ourselves as capable, and therefore our outlook is optimistic. The opposite can also be true. If we don't believe we can successfully pass an exam then our self-efficacy is low, this in turn affects our self-esteem because we see ourselves as a failure and our outlook becomes pessimistic.

Answer the following questions:

1 How does self-regulation work?

2 What is the meaning of self-efficacy?

3 How can punishment lead to the learning of unwanted behaviours?

Progress exercise

## Evaluation

The core studies that enabled Bandura to theorise about social learning theory are the bobo doll experiments mentioned earlier (see Box 5.1 for an example). Therefore, evaluations of his theory tend to focus on these studies.

The bobo doll experiments were carried out periodically from 1961 to 1977. Most of the studies involved the use of filmed models (the

1961 study consisted of the only live model) initiating aggressive-type behaviours towards a bobo doll. In each study the behaviour was then shown to a group of children who were later observed to see if they would imitate the behaviour of the model, which would indicate that learning had taken place. This did seem to be the case in a significant number of the studies. As pointed out by Baron (1977), these studies could be seen as highlighting the negative effect TV can have on the behaviour of children which may be contributing to the ever-increasing levels of violence in society today. However, others have pointed out that the studies themselves are not flawless and can be criticised in a number of ways. These will now be considered under separate headings.

## Realism

One criticism of the bobo doll studies is lack of realism. For example, the object towards which the violence was directed was a plastic doll. Although Bandura found that the children did reproduce the behaviour they had witnessed, Baron (1977) argues that it would be more appropriate to interpret the behaviour as a form of play, rather than as aggressive behaviour that should cause concern. Also, as noted by Gross (1990), the context in which the aggressive behaviour was observed was not one in which the children would normally find themselves. For example, the material observed by the children in the various studies differed in many ways from standard TV viewing. First, the presentation time was very brief (approximately 3.5 mins); most TV programmes are a lot longer. Second, there was no plot to provide justification for the behaviour of the social model, whereas children's TV programmes tend to have a storyline (however simple) that the child can follow. Last, the behaviour shown was very bizarre (an adult aggressing towards a plastic doll) and not likely to be something children would watch on TV. All of these points undermine the **ecological validity** of Bandura's research and cast doubt on whether the media is in fact contributing to the increasing violence in society today.

However, there is also lots of evidence to support Bandura's findings, and show that children often use play as a tool for learning. A study conducted by Johnson et al. (1977, cited in Baron 1977) found that the amount of aggressive play initiated by children at nursery school was significantly related to ratings of their general aggression by peers and teachers. Bandura himself (1977) describes how aggressive behaviour is often learned in environments that are far removed from reality, and gives the example of a boxer training to fight using a punch bag or a hunter practising shooting at targets. However, as pointed out by Cumberbatch (1990), the novelty of knocking down a toy that bounces back each time is a highly pleasurable activity. He shows that children who had never experienced a bobo doll before were five times more likely to imitate aggressive behaviour against it, than those who had experienced it before. Therefore, to conclude, the aggression shown towards the bobo doll was due to the pleasure gained from the toy, rather than imitative aggression.

### *Media influences*

Since Bandura's original studies, lots of research into the possible negative effects of TV programmes on behaviour have been carried out with varying results. A longitudinal study by Eron (1982), found that the amount of TV violence watched at a young age was positively correlated with the amount of aggression shown in adulthood (measured by number of criminal convictions by age 30). This indicates that watching violent TV programmes may be a factor in subsequent aggressive behaviour.

Comstock and Paik (1991), after reviewing the findings of 1000 studies on the effects of media violence, concluded that there are strong short-term effects and weaker long-term effects. They put forward five factors that appear to increase the likelihood of aggressive behaviour from watching TV:

1 The viewer identifies with the person behaving violently.
2 The violent behaviour being observed is realistic (as opposed to a cartoon). This point raises the issue of realism in the bobo doll studies.
3 The suffering of the victims is not shown.
4 The violent behaviour being shown causes the viewer to become emotionally excited.
5 Violent behaviour is presented as being an effective way of getting what one wants.

However, more recent research by Charlton (1998), found that the inhabitants of the island of St Helena, who only received television in 1995, had not experienced any increases in violent behaviour since that time. If we assume that some of the programmes viewed would have depicted violent scenes, then this shows that watching violent TV need not lead to increased levels of aggression.

Finally, one of the few cross-cultural studies by Huesmann and Eron (1986), observed adults and children over a three-year period in Poland, Finland, Israel and Australia. Findings were that the amount of TV violence observed by children was highly correlated with their subsequent levels of aggression in three of the chosen countries. However, for Australia this effect did not occur. The conclusion drawn was that generally media violence does indeed increase aggressive behaviour.

In terms of Bandura's social learning theory, it seems that children can and do learn to behave aggressively from exposure to violent models. However, this effect is not as straightforward as first thought, and other factors (as shown by the above studies) must be taken into account before a way forward can be proposed.

## Mischel's theory of personality

Walter Mischel, in agreement with Bandura, believes that much of our personality is learned through our interaction with the environment. He also emphasises (again like Bandura) how cognitive factors play a major role in determining an individual's behaviour and the consequences of that behaviour; this is what Bandura calls reciprocal determinism.

However Mischel adds a further dimension to his theory by arguing that individual differences in the way we think and therefore behave, create differences in personalities. In other words, put in the same situation two people would behave very differently due to a variety of personal differences. Mischel calls these differences **person variables**. The following are the most significant:

1 *Expectancies*: based on our life experiences, our past behaviour and our knowledge of current situations, we have particular expectations about the effect our behaviour will have. Perhaps in the past we have worked as a waiter/waitress in a restaurant and have learned that by being friendly we are more likely to be left a good tip. Therefore, if we find ourselves in a similar situation, we feel we know how to behave in order to gain the most profitable outcome.

2 *Subjective values*: we value some outcomes above others and it is towards these valued outcomes that we will strive. For example, we may place a high value on achieving a particular grade in a specific subject we are studying and this will obviously have an effect on how we behave e.g. we study hard, attend all lessons etc.

3 *Cognitive strategies*: the way we interpret and process incoming information also has an effect on our behaviour. An example of this might be our reaction to an invitation to a party: where one person may see this as an exciting prospect, another may be filled with dread, while a third person may interpret the information as dull and be uninterested.

4 *Competencies*: we have different skills and abilities that have a bearing on how we behave in particular situations. An individual with very good social skills, for example, will behave very differently at a party than someone who is shy and inhibited.

5 *Self-regulatory systems and plans*: this final person variable is similar to Bandura's concept of self-regulation, whereby we constantly monitor our behaviour and either reward or punish ourselves depending on our progress towards our aspirations. We also change and modify our behaviour in line with reaching our goals most effectively.

These five person variables contribute to each individual's unique way of approaching life and they form the core of Mischel's personality theory. However, the way a person approaches life is constantly changing as they learn and experience different things and adjust and readjust their behaviour accordingly. For this reason Mischel's theory is a dynamic one as it not only accounts for individual differences in behaviour, but allows for the constantly changing social and personal interactions that take place in all our lives and continually effect and re-effect the person we are.

Make a list of Mischel's five person variables and for each one give an example of how you would behave in a specific situation.

Review exercise

## Evaluation

How does Mischel's personality theory differ from other personality theories such as Allport's trait theory, which also postulates individual differences in personalities? The main difference seems to be the emphasis each theorist places on the basis of personality or how personality evolves. Allport argues that personality traits are a unique part of a person's makeup or temperament, thereby emphasising the biological or innate basis of personality. Mischel, in agreement with Bandura, believes that personality is more to do with our past learning experiences and how these interact with (and so have an effect on) our present way of thinking (our cognitions). The basis of personality according to Mischel, therefore, is the interaction between cognition and situation.

### Can we predict behaviour?

Social learning theorists such as Mischel (1968, 1976) argue that individual personality is not consistent across situations, and for this reason using traits to predict behaviour is a waste of time, believing instead that a good predictor of behaviour is often the situation a person finds themselves in. This can be seen clearly if we take two very different situations, for example, the birth of a child and the funeral of a loved one. We can see that whatever personality traits a person has been categorised as possessing, they will behave very differently at the birth than they will at the funeral. Knowing that a person is sociable and ambitious will not help us to predict their behaviour in either of the two situations. The situations themselves would have far more effect on the behaviour of the individual, and so would be more reliable as a predictor. However, others have argued that situation is not always the best predictor of behaviour. Zuckerman (1991) points out that although some situations constrain behaviour such as the examples given above, others permit a wide variety of responses. He gives the example of traffic light signals, and particularly the amber traffic light. Given the amber light some drivers may slow down and stop if possible, while others will speed up and accelerate through the light. In this case the personality of the individual would be more predictive of behaviour than the situation.

## Conclusion

It seems that to focus on either situation or personality alone as a predictor of behaviour is to oversimplify the issue. Many theorists point out that an **interactionist** approach that stresses the influence of both situation and individual personality is the best predictor of behaviour. Social learning theorists, although opposed to using personality traits to predict behaviour, probably come the closest to this position as they focus on the interaction between the individual's cognition (or person variables in the case of Mischel) and the environment.

Overall, social learning theory has been most influential in explaining how children and adults learn through observing others and so develop their personalities. Although Bandura agrees that biological factors can affect personality, he stresses the importance of situation and experience in predicting behaviour.

## Summary

In this chapter we have discussed and evaluated two personality theories that focus on the environment as having an effect on personality. First, we have discussed in detail the ideas of Albert Bandura, who felt that the explanations of human behaviour advocated by the behaviourist school of thought were too simplistic. This led him to develop his own theory of learning known as social learning theory. We have gone on to describe the experimental bobo doll studies that formed the basis of evidence for this theory. We have also covered in detail specific factors that shape our personalities according to Bandura, such as reciprocal determinism (the way we affect and are affected by the environment), and self-regulation. Finally, we have evaluated Bandura's theory of personality by reviewing several studies that provide both evidence and criticism. In the second part of this chapter we have discussed an alternative social learning theory of personality put forward by Walter Mischel. In agreement with Bandura, Mischel highlights the interaction of the environment and the individual, but adds a further factor of individual differences or 'person variables' as creating differences in personality. We have evaluated Mischel's ideas and have gone on to examine the implications of social learning theory in relation to the media. Finally, we have concluded that individual personality appears to be the product of both internal and external factors.

## Further Reading

Grusec, J.E. (1992) Social learning theory and developmental psychology: the legacies of Robert Sears and Albert Bandura. *Developmental Psychology* 28, 776–786. An in-depth look at Bandura's theory, both historical and applied.

Horowitz, F.D. (1992) John B. Watson's legacy: learning and environment. *Developmental Psychology* 28, 360–376. The foundations of learning theory – interesting and informative.

# Section II

## GENDER
## DEVELOPMENT

# 6

# Social and biological approaches to gender identity

### Definition of gender

Previous chapters have shown how psychologists have attempted to explain who we are as individuals through descriptions of our personality. Some theorists believe our behaviours are largely genetically inherited (e.g. Eysenck) while others emphasise the effect society has on our behaviour (e.g. Bandura). An alternative to this perspective is to consider behaviour in terms of gender.

By gender we mean masculinity and femininity, the trappings that go along with being a particular sex, rather than the sex itself. The *Concise Oxford Dictionary* defines gender as 'the grammatical classification of nouns and related words, roughly corresponding to the two sexes and sexlessness'. Gender thus relates to aspects such as role in society, preferences for particular activities, typical sexual orientation and so on. Gender has a major impact on who we are and how we behave; it perhaps overrides all other influences.

The biological differences between the sexes originate in our genes. Human cells have forty-six chromosomes which hold the genetic material DNA; twenty-three of these chromosomes are inherited from our mother, and twenty-three from our father. These are arranged as twenty-three pairs of chromosomes, and the twenty-third pair, the so-called sex chromosomes, determine the biological sex of the child. In females the twenty-third chromosome pair consists of two essentially identical 'X' chromosomes. In males, however, one of the X chromosomes is replaced by a smaller 'Y' chromosome.

Historically, this biological fact led to the common-sense view that if sex is genetically predetermined in this way, then so is gender (Deaux 1985). The degree to which this is so is considered throughout the remainder of the chapter.

## Gender identity and sex role stereotypes

An individual's **gender identity** is their sense of being male or female and of belonging to that particular group in society. It is thought we acquire our gender identity through a process of socialisation known as **sex typing**, that takes account of the separate roles expected of males and females in our society. These separate roles are called **gender roles** or **sex role stereotypes**. A stereotype according to Wrightsman (1977) is 'a relatively rigid and oversimplified conception of a group of people in which all individuals in the group are labelled with the so-called group characteristics'. In other words, we believe certain things about particular groups of people. For example, in Western societies, females are traditionally expected to be nurturing and caring in readiness for their role as wife and/or mother, when they will organise and care for the family. Males are expected to be ambitious and competitive, as their role involves providing for the family and protecting them. These roles appear to be culturally prescribed and therefore are likely to be learned rather than innate. Eagley (1987) suggests that: 'Gender roles are those shared expectations (of behaviour) that apply to individuals on the basis of their socially identified gender'. In Western societies these expectations act to narrow the life options for males by prescribing roles that are fairly rigid. For example, it is more deviant for a male to take on a traditional female role such as that of homemaker, secretary or midwife, than it is for a female to take on a traditional male role such as that of a lorry driver, plumber or doctor. However in Western society the female gender role in comparison with the male gender role has less value and carries less self-esteem and prestige. For example, the role of housewife is perceived to be of lower status than company executive.

---

1  Give a definition of the term gender.

2  Using the definition given by the *Oxford Dictionary*, try to explain what gender means.

3  Explain what is meant by the concept of gender identity.

4  What is sex typing?

5  Give two examples of how sex typing occurs in Western society.

*Progress exercise*

---

### The effects of sex role stereotypes on behaviour

One way of trying to understand how and why sex stereotypes come about is to consider actual sex differences in behaviour. However, a difficulty here is in trying to determine to what extent a gender difference is caused by the effects of sex role stereotyping on our expectations of male and female behaviour. For example, Sherman (1983) examined the intellectual development of females in comparison with males, and stated that, 'data indicate that intellectual excellence is still enmeshed in a pattern of sex role expectations contrary to the feminine sex role'. In other words, the effects of sex role stereotyping is so pervasive in our culture, that (using the example of intellect) any female striving to reach her intellectual potential runs the risk of behaving in a manner that is not expected and generally not encouraged for her gender. Therefore, trying to determine the extent to which a gender difference is being influenced by stereotyping is extremely difficult, and raises a fundamental question about gender differences. Is it the sex role stereotype that creates an expectation of behaviour that then leads to differences (almost like a **self-fulfilling prophesy**)? Or are there actual gender differences that have led to the development of sex role stereotypes?

Some people might argue that in today's Western culture the roles of males and females have become more equal, and therefore the effect of sex role stereotypes have become weaker. However, as a survey by Skelton (1990) illustrates, people still differentiate between the genders when describing their general behaviours. For example, Skelton found that positive descriptions of female politicians focused on their being 'hardworking', 'more caring' and 'more ethical', whereas male politicians were seen as 'tougher' and 'more emotionally suited to politics'. As a particularly well-known example, Prime Minister Margaret Thatcher, whose behaviour was often opposite to the expected female sex role, was frequently described in gender terms as being an 'honorary male'.

**Progress exercise**

Do sex role stereotypes continue to effect our behaviour in contemporary society? Ask some of your friends (male and female) to answer the following questions (taken from a questionnaire by Jonides and Rozin (1981), and see if you can detect a sex-related difference in their answers:

1  Would you be willing to kill a cockroach by slapping it with your hands?

2  When you are depressed does washing your hair make you feel better?

3  Can you sew well enough to make clothes?

4  Do you enjoy shopping?

### Research evidence applied to gender differences

In 1974 Eleanor Maccoby and Carolyn Jacklin carried out a meta-analysis of more than 1500 studies claiming to show differences between the sexes. They concluded that most gender differences are a fallacy. In fact, of the many gender differences originally postulated they found just four that at that time continued to be significant. These were verbal ability, visual/spatial abilities, mathematical ability and aggression. However more recent research provides a changing picture. See Table 6.1 for a summary of the most recent findings.

Jacklin (1989) found that boys are also more likely than girls to show a variety of developmental disorders, such as reading disabilities, speech impediments, hyperactivity and emotional disorders. More recent research by Maccoby (1990) has found other differences between the genders. For example, girls are generally more compliant

**Table 6.1** The four gender differences supported by Maccoby and Jacklin (1974)

| Gender differences | Experimental evidence |
|---|---|
| *Verbal ability* | • Maccoby and Jacklin found that females have greater verbal ability than males. Girls develop verbal skills at an earlier age than boys, and perform better on tests of reading comprehension and speech fluency.<br>• However, research by Feingold (1988) found that the difference in performance on verbal tests between girls and boys is so small that it can no longer be considered to be significant. |
| *Visual/spatial abilities* | • Maccoby and Jacklin argue that traditionally males were thought to outperform females on tests that required either inferences to be drawn from, or mental manipulation of, pictorial information.<br>• Kerns and Berenbaun (1991) found in contemporary society that, although these gender differences do still exist, they are very small. |
| *Mathematical ability* | • Maccoby and Jacklin argue that starting in adolescence boys appear to have an advantage over girls on tests of arithmetic reasoning. This evidence is supported by Feingold (1988).<br>• Interestingly, Feingold (1992) found that more boys than girls are exceptionally good at maths, but also more boys than girls are exceptionally poor at maths.<br>• However, Brynes and Takahira (1993) found that girls exceed boys in computational skills. |
| *Aggression* | • Maccoby and Jacklin found that males were more verbally and physically aggressive than females.<br>• According to Eagley and Steffen (1986) this finding has not changed significantly since then. |

than boys to requests from teachers, parents and authority figures. Girls are also more likely to rely on tact and polite suggestions, rather than force or demand, when attempting to persuade others to comply with them. Lastly, girls are more interested in, and show more sensitivity towards, infants (Reid, Tate and Berman 1989).

In reviewing the evidence for gender differences it is worth bearing in mind that the findings given are based on data that reflects group averages, and so may not be applicable to any particular individual. Also gender differences that appear in one social context, or in a particular culture, may not show up elsewhere (Daubman, Heatherington and Ahn 1992). For example, research by Baker and Jones (1992) found that in Israel women perform significantly better on tests of mathematical ability than do men. This is contrary to the sex role stereotype concerning mathematical ability found in Western cultures, whereby males are expected to outperform females. Thus, some gender differences are not only culturally specific, but do indeed (as noted earlier in the chapter) set up expectations of appropriate behaviour that often lead to differences in performance.

## Social learning theory

In Chapter 5 we discussed Bandura's social learning theory in terms of personality development, and saw how our personality can be shaped by the social world in which we live. Our life experiences have an impact on how we react to, and interact with, the world around us. This in turn affects how we deal with each new experience we have, thereby helping to create the person we eventually become.

Linked to the development of our personality is our gradual awareness of our gender. According to social learning theory, gender identity (like personality) is sensitive to the type of behaviour we are exposed to, both at home and in the social world. Social learning theorists believe we build up our gender identity through a process of modelling and differential reinforcement.

### Modelling

As children develop and learn they are constantly being exposed to models of sex-typed behaviour. In a traditional home a child may see their mother carrying out household chores such as washing, cleaning and cooking while their father is at work. They will probably go shopping with their mother while their father may be more involved in maintenance around the home. Leisure pursuits such as attending football matches or race circuits may also be seen as male sex-typed behaviour. However this is not always the case and the changing roles of males and females in Western society today may lead to a reversal in these traditional roles. Maybe dad does the shopping, while mum takes the kids to a football match. Or perhaps there is only one parent at home, who takes on the traditional roles of both genders. Whatever the case, social learning theorists believe that one of the ways children learn gender roles is by modelling their own behaviour on the behaviour they experience at home (Turner and Gervai 1995).

*The experiments of Perry and Bussey*

Although on its own modelling may be too simplistic an explanation of how a child might acquire its gender identity, it can be seen as a contributory factor. Perry and Bussey (1979) carried out some experiments to investigate the extent modelling has on gender development:

*Experiment 1*: In this first experiment children observed four female and four male models selecting an item from a choice of two (e.g. they could choose between an apple and a banana). The children were then asked which item they themselves would prefer. Findings were that if all four of the female models chose the same item, and all four of the male models chose the other one, then the children tended to choose the item that the model who was the same sex as themselves had chosen. If however only two of the female models and two of the male models chose the same item and the other two pairs of models chose the other item, then the children tended to choose indiscriminately (see Figure 6.1). This shows that children will only imitate the behaviour of a same-sex model if the behaviour shown by the model is the most frequently performed behaviour for models of that gender. So, for example, a child who is exposed to a model performing a behaviour which is not normally seen in that gender, e.g. a man wearing a dress, then the child will not necessarily imitate that behaviour.

*Experiment 2*: Again the children observed four female and four male models, but in this experiment three of the female models and one of the male models chose the same item, while the other three male models and one female model chose the other. As the four models in each group chose the same item the children were able to observe that one male and one female model were behaving sex inappropriately in relation to the behaviour of the other three. When asked which item they themselves would prefer the children were significantly more likely to imitate the behaviour of the three same-sex models than the single model of either sex (see Figure 6.1). This again indicates that modelling has an effect on gender development only if the behaviours observed are seen by the observer as typical behaviours for that sex (are sex-appropriate behaviours). Sex-appropriate behaviours appear to be those behaviours that are performed by the majority of models of the same sex.

*Experiment 1*

| four females = four bananas | four males = four apples |
|---|---|
| two females + two males = four bananas | two females + two males = four apples |

*Experiment 2*

| three males + one female = four bananas | three females + one male = four apples |
|---|---|

*Figure 6.1* **Perry and Bussey's experimental conditions**

To conclude, it seems that children learn gender-appropriate behaviour from models they perceive as acting in a sex-appropriate way. Whether or not a behaviour is seen as sex-appropriate is determined by the frequency that the child sees a member of their *own sex* performing that behaviour.

## Differential reinforcement

Differential reinforcement simply means that different behaviours are reinforced according to gender. For example, boys and girls are dressed differently and given different toys to play with (Pomerleau et al. 1990). Also, it is often thought that boys are handled more roughly and receive more physical discipline than girls, while girls are treated in a more gentle manner and are less likely to be physically punished. Other types of differential reinforcement include the type of interests children are encouraged to take up.

## Observations by Beverley Fagot

Fagot (1978) carried out an observation study of twenty-four American families each with a child aged between 20 and 24 months old. She visited the homes of the families in order to observe the parents interacting with their children in a natural setting. Each visit lasted approximately an hour and every family received five visits. Fagot was looking for examples of differential reinforcement, such as girls being encouraged in any type of behaviour that boys were discouraged in, and vice versa. Fagot found very clear instances of differential reinforcement in the way parents responded to their offspring. For example, girls were encouraged to dance, to play with dolls, to stay near the parent and to ask for help. They were discouraged from climbing, jumping and running, and from participating in any type of overly active or rough play. They were also discouraged from manipulating objects and from exploring. Boys on the other hand were positively encouraged to take part in rough play, to run and jump and to explore their environment. They were encouraged to manipulate objects and to play with sex-appropriate toys such as trucks, cars or building blocks. However, boys were discouraged and sometimes even punished for taking part in what were seen as feminine activities such as playing with dolls, dancing and asking for help.

Fagot also found that fathers were more likely to encourage their daughters to stay close and not to explore, and to criticise their sons for playing with dolls. Mothers on the other hand were more likely to encourage their sons to explore and their daughters to help them in day-to-day activities.

Overall, Fagot's observations indicate that differential reinforcement has a large impact on the development of gender identity. Boys and girls are treated differently from a very young age and this leads to an early acceptance of the type of gender appropriate behaviour expected of them. Other studies with similar findings include: Weitzman, Birns and Friend (1985) and Weisner and Wilson-Mitchell (1990).

Fagot and Leinbach (1987) further note that the way children are dressed serves to reinforce gender role expectations, by the way others respond to them. They argue that gender-type clothing not only serves to differentiate boys and girls, but also ensures that strangers will respond to the child in ways that are considered appropriate for his or her gender.

1 Explain the meaning of the terms modelling and differential reinforcement.

2 Provide evidence that both modelling and differential reinforcement are involved in the learning of gender identity.

## Other research into the effects of social models

Other research has looked at the degree to which children imitate the characteristics of their parent/parents, and the wider effect of this on the process of sex-typing. Turner and Gervai (1995) conducted a study and found that those parents who are highly traditional in their gender roles, have children who are highly sex typed. Further evidence of the pervasive role of parents comes from a study by Ruble and Martin (1998). They found that whether parents are traditional or not, the way they behave has a strong impact on the development of their children's gender roles and behaviour. As the structure of the 'normal' family today is not necessarily made up of two opposite-sex parents, research in this area has also focused on whether the absence of one or other parent has any detrimental effects on the development of gender identity. Findings indicate that boys are more likely to have problems with their gender identity if a male figure is not available, whether this is a temporary or permanent situation (Ruble and Martin 1998). However, other studies that have focused on the children of gay or lesbian households have challenged the importance of the father's contribution to gender typing. Patterson (1992) found that children raised in lesbian households did not differ in gender role behaviour from those raised in heterosexual households. Similarly, Bailey, Bobrow, Wolfe and Mikach (1995) found that boys raised by gay fathers still showed traditional gender role behaviour. These findings seem to indicate that although parents play a part in this process children learn their gender roles from a variety of sources.

## Evaluation

The findings of Beverley Fagot's observational study of young children and their parents, and Perry and Bussey's experiments on modelling, both indicate (along with many other contemporary studies cited above) that social learning plays a major role in reinforcing sex-appropriate behaviour. This behaviour eventually forms part of the gender identity that each child develops as they grow into adulthood. However, social pressures such as differential reinforcement and modelling may not be the only determinants of gender-appropriate behaviour.

Some theorists argue that although social learning contributes to the development of gender identity, the main explanation of gendered behaviour is due to biological differences that predispose males and females to behave in ways particular to their sex (see Hines 1993). This biological model puts forward the argument that, genetically, men have a greater physical strength which makes them better as hunters and explorers, while in contrast women's capacity to bear children puts them in more nurturant roles. These separate roles of males and females then work together, complementing each other, to produce a strong and successful species. However, this argument is very **deterministic** as it defines the separate roles of males and females in a way that allows no flexibility or redefinition. In this way people are seen almost as victims of their gender, with no alternative ways of behaving or identity available other than that predetermined by their genes. This view highlights the nature/nurture debate prevalent in all areas of psychology, with the emphasis firmly on the nature side of the argument.

### Biosocial theory

An alternative to seeing gender identity as either directly due to biology or purely down to social influences, is to see it as an interaction of both. From this stance John Money and Anke Ehrhardt (1972) have proposed biosocial theory. This theory emphasises the role of biology in directing and constraining development, but acknowledges the role of socialisation in guiding a child towards a particular gender identity.

Money and Ehrhardt's theory consists of a number of critical steps that contribute to an individual's final preference for a masculine or feminine identity. These are as follows:

1   Once conceived a child inherits either an X or a Y chromosome from their father which determines whether the embryo develops testes or ovaries.

2 Once this step is achieved the newly-developed testes secrete two hormones: *testosterone*, which stimulates the development of the male internal reproductive system, and *mullerian inhibiting substance* (MIS) which inhibits the development of female reproductive organs. If these hormones are absent the internal reproductive system of the female develops.

3 At about 4 months after conception a third critical step occurs: the secretion of testosterone by the testes leads to the development of a penis and scrotum. If testosterone is absent (as in females), or if the male foetus has inherited a rare genetic disorder known as **testicular feminization syndrome** (TFS), in which his body is insensitive to the male hormone, external female genitalia will develop.

4 Once the biological male or female is born social influences begin to play a part, according to the appearance of his or her genitalia. If the genitalia of the newborn baby is abnormal, the infant will be labelled according to the sex he or she most closely resembles, and will be treated as such. If the child happens to be a boy suffering from TFS, he may well be treated as a girl for a considerable period of time. This erroneous labelling would have an effect on his gender identity. Money and Ehrhardt believe that children acquire an early infant gender identity at approximately 3 years of age.

5 Once the child reaches puberty, biological factors again begin to have an effect. Large quantities of hormones are released and stimulate the growth of the reproductive system, as well as the emergence of secondary sex characteristics (e.g. deepening of the voice in males and changing body shape in females) and the development of sexual urges. Combined with the child's earlier self-concept as a male or female, these biological changes provide the basis of an adult gender identity.

## Evaluation

What evidence is there that biosocial theory is correct in assuming that an individual's gender identity is formed from an interaction of biological and social influences? We have already considered during the first part of this chapter the effects of socialisation on the child's self-concept, but what about biological evidence?

During the 1970s women who were experiencing difficult pregnancies were given drugs containing progestins, which are converted into the male hormone testosterone as they enter the body. These drugs acted to masculinize the female foetuses, so that the child was born with genitalia resembling that of a male. For example, the clitoris was very enlarged (like a penis) and the labia fused (like a scrotum). Money and Erhardt (1972) observed many of these masculinized females who had subsequently undergone surgery altering the appearance of their genitalia to resemble that of a female. They were then raised as females, but from the beginning displayed tomboyish behaviour. They would often play with boys, showing a preference for boy's toys and boy's activities over those traditionally favoured by girls. During adolescence they began dating later than their peers, and felt that marriage should be delayed until they had established themselves in their careers. A high percentage of these females (37 per cent) described themselves as homosexual or bisexual (Money 1985).

This observation suggests that early exposure to male hormones can have a masculinizing effect on a female foetus, leading to the development of male-like behaviours. This may effect the eventual gender identity of the individual. However, some of the females in the sample had received cortisone therapy to prevent further masculinization of their bodies, and one side-effect of cortisone is to dramatically raise an individual's activity level. Therefore, an alternative explanation may be that the patterns of behaviour displayed by the females were due more to the cortisone than to their prenatal exposure to the male sex hormones (Huston 1983).

A different study focusing on the impact of biological influences on gender identity concerns a 21-month-old male identical twin whose penis was accidently damaged beyond repair during circumcision (Money and Tucker 1975). After considering the alternatives his parents decided on a surgical procedure that would turn their son into a girl anatomically. Note that as the child was not yet 2 years old, this was within Ehrhardt and Money's critical period during which gender identity is acquired. Once the operation was complete the family began to treat the boy like a girl, dressing him in female clothing, changing his hairstyle and buying female-appropriate toys. By 5 years of age the child knew that she was a girl, she had developed a preference for feminine toys and activities. She was now very different from her identical twin brother, being far daintier and neater.

It seemed that this was a case where sex role socialisation had overcome biological predisposition. However, in 1982, when BBC presenter Milton Diamond carried out a follow-up programme on the case, he found that by age 13 the female twin was not as well adjusted as previously thought. According to her psychiatrists she was seriously maladjusted. She felt unhappy and uncomfortable in her female role, and had been rejected by her peers who had labelled her 'cavewoman'. This may have been partly due to her somewhat masculine appearance, which persisted despite her taking estrogen to prevent further masculinization of her body. By the time she reached adulthood she had totally rejected her female identity and had reverted to that of a male. A further BBC follow-up programme found the twin married and in the process of undergoing surgical procedures to re-establish external male genitalia.

This case seems to provide strong evidence for the role of biology in the development of gender identity. It also provides evidence against Money and Ehrhardt's idea that a critical period exists, up to age 3, when a child can be socialised as either gender. It seems that the first three years of life are more of a sensitive period than a critical one, as in this case biology overrode the socialization experienced by the child during this time.

**Progress exercise**

1  Note down the five critical steps of biosocial theory put forward by Money and Erhardt.

2  Describe two pieces of evidence for and against this theory.

## Cross-cultural studies

Comparing the gender role behaviours of people from different cultures is a further way of determining the extent to which gender identity is the result of socialization or biology (nature or nurture). Many studies have been carried out and findings seem to indicate (as is often the case) that *both* play a role in the development of gender identity.

## The work of Margaret Mead

The cross-cultural work of anthropologist Margaret Mead has highlighted the great effect culture has on the behaviour of people. Mead was the first researcher to conduct psychologically-oriented field work and to link psychology to the discipline of anthropology. This encouraged researchers in other areas such as ethology and sociology to consider the impact of culture on behaviour, and opened up whole new areas of research in the race to understand humanity.

Mead's first study took place in Samoa in 1923, where she observed the behaviour of Samoan female adolescents and compared their behaviour with American female adolescents. From this research Mead found differences as well as similarities in behaviour, and concluded that culture rather than genes was the reason. The gender-appropriate behaviour expected of adolescent girls growing up in Samoa and adolescent girls growing up in America in terms of the nurturing role they play is very similar, but in other ways (such as academic ability) is very different.

A further study in New Guinea (1931) provided more evidence of the influence culture has on the behaviour of people. During this study Mead observed three different cultural groups (the Arapesh, the Mundugumor and the Tchambuli), and found wide varieties in the gender-appropriate behaviour of each group. The males and females of the Arapesh culture were highly equal. They took turns in looking after the children and in practical everyday tasks such as food gathering, cooking and cleaning. They appeared to be a non-aggressive society and lived in harmony with one another. The Mundugumor on the other hand were a much fiercer society who displayed high levels of aggressive behaviour, both towards their own people and to outsiders. Mundugumor children were often left to fend for themselves at very young ages (4–5 years old), and it was common practise to cast infants of the wrong sex into the river to drown. The final cultural group that Mead studied were the Tchambuli people who in comparison with Western culture appeared to show a role reversal in sex-appropriate behaviour. For example, males were expected to take care of the children and run the household. They were also encouraged to be creative and sentimental. Males could often be found in groups, gossiping and making themselves look pretty. Females on the other hand were competitive and efficient, they conducted all matters to do with trade and commerce and were responsible for all decisions concerning the running of the village. The life of the Tchambuli male revolved around that of the female.

## Evaluation

The various studies involving social learning, hormonal influences and cross-cultural research that we have discussed throughout this chapter have illustrated the interaction of biology and learning on the behaviour and gender identities acquired by males and females. Although some theorists believe that biology/genes are the basis of all gendered behaviours, it has been shown that learning also plays a role in determining the type of behaviour each gender exhibits. The work of Fagot, Perry and Bussey and many others has upheld social learning theory as an explanation of how children learn gender appropriate behaviours and develop their gender identities, while the research of Money and Ehrhardt as well as many others has illustrated the sometimes overriding effects of biology. Finally, cross-cultural research such as that carried out by Margaret Mead has reiterated the great impact of culture on our internalisation of appropriate gender behaviours.

## Summary

As the first chapter in the gender development section we have started by defining what we mean by gender and gender identity along with other relevant terms, such as sex-typing and gender roles. We have discussed how the term *gender* differs from the term *sex* in that the latter refers mainly to physiological aspects, whereas the other is gained through an interaction of many factors, including learning and biological predisposition. We have gone on to discuss the ideas of social learning theorists concerning the ways we develop our gender identities, and have reviewed evidence that indicates learning is not the only factor. In view of this we have discussed biological theories of gender identity, and again have reviewed the evidence both for and against this perspective. Finally, we have concluded that overall findings suggest that both biology and learning, in varying degrees, play a role in shaping the gender identity each of us eventually attain.

## Further reading

Gerson, K. (1985) *Hard choices: how women decide about work, motherhood and career*, Berkeley: University of California Press. For those with a particular interest in this area this book provides an in-depth look at the many factors women must consider if they wish to have children and also work.

Pilcher, J. (1999) *Women in contemporary Britain*, London: Routledge. An up-to-date discussion of the social and psychological constraints facing women today.

Segal, L. (1990) *Slow motion: changing masculinities, changing men*, London: Virago. Discussions about the way the male role and masculinity is changing in today's society.

# 7

# Cognitive development theories

## Cognitive development theories

Along with social learning theories, cognitive development theories emphasise the social world (rather than the influence of biology) as having an impact on the development of gender identity. These theories emphasise the active role people play in the process of development by depicting the person as actively instrumental in trying to make sense of the world around him or her. However, unlike social learning theories, cognitive developmentalists believe that children develop through various stages, and each stage brings with it a different level of comprehension or ability to think and reason. This means that at any given time a child will only possess the abilities to make sense of, or draw conclusions about the world, at the level (or stage) of development they are currently at. For example, a very young child at an early stage of cognitive development may learn that boys and girls are different because of the way they look (e.g. girls wear dresses). If they are then faced with a boy wearing a dress, they will automatically assume that he must be a she because of how he looks. They will have no reason to question this assumption, as the stage of cognitive development they are at uses only particular aspects (in this case visual perception) to judge a situation, or to make sense of the world. At a later stage the child will begin to use a wider range of skills from which to draw conclusions about situations. For example, they will learn that the way something looks (its superficial features) can change without affecting its true identity. In this way children learn through this active construction of the world which gender identity and therefore gender role is appropriate for them.

## Kohlberg's theory of gender development

Kohlberg's (1966) theory of gender development grew out of the work of the Swiss psychologist Jean Piaget. As one of the first theorists to seriously examine the way children think and reason, Piaget's theory of cognitive development not only was to have far-reaching effects on the way Western children were educated, but also led to a mass of research in the 1960s and 1970s. Piaget believed children's thought processes go through various stages of development as the child matures. He assumed that children initially focus on the surface appearance of things in order to make sense of them (for example, a dog has four legs therefore any animal with four legs must be a dog) and only later begin to look beyond what they perceive visually. Empirical evidence has shown this assumption to be correct, and it is this part of Piaget's theory that has relevance to Kohlberg's beliefs about gender.

According to Kohlberg (1966) a child's understanding of gender roles and gender identity evolves through three stages of cognitive development: gender labelling, gender stability and gender constancy.

### Gender labelling

At about the age of 2 years children enter the gender labelling stage where they become aware of their own and others gender. Prior to this stage they have no concept of gender as a way of categorising themselves or others. However by the age of 2 they are able to consistently label themselves and others as male or female. In order to achieve this differentiation between the sexes the child relies on its perception of the physical characteristics of others. The way a person dresses, their hair, or even the activities they perform can inform the child of the other's gender. For example, somebody wearing a suit and tie with short hair would be seen as male, while a person wearing a dress and having long hair would be seen as female. If these characteristics change, for example the man grows his hair long, then the gender changes too. Although the child is now aware of gender and can categorise people as male or female, their reliance on superficial features as a way of judging sex means that to them gender is not a static concept. In other words, to a 2-year-old child gender does not necessarily stay the same throughout life, but can change as often as a person changes their physical appearance.

### Gender stability

At approximately 3 to 4 years of age the child's perception of gender begins to change and they move into the gender stability stage. Now the child is aware that a person remains the same gender for life. They realise that boys grow up to be men, and girls grow up to be women. Their own gender becomes salient to them, and they embrace gender-appropriate activities while shunning activities that are inappropriate for their gender according to the cultural norm. However, although children at this stage understand that gender is stable across time (we grow up to be the same gender we are as children), they still have not grasped that gender is also stable across situations. The child still retains the belief that a person's gender might change if they engage in gender-inappropriate behaviour, such as a boy playing with dolls, or a girl playing with cars.

### Gender constancy

At around 5 years of age the child reaches the stage where they understand that gender is an unchanging part of our identity, both across time and situation. They perceive gender as an underlying part of us that is stable regardless of activities engaged in, or clothes worn. They no longer judge gender on superficial characteristics, as they realise that features like hair and clothing etc. are irrelevant to the true gender identity of the person. Interestingly, the accomplishment of the gender constancy stage occurs around the same age as Piaget's concept of **conservation**, whereby the child realises that changing the shape of an object does not necessarily change its mass. For example, a child who can conserve will know that a tall thin glass holds as much liquid as a short fat glass even though they appear very different. Likewise a child who has reached the gender constancy stage will know that a person with short hair and wearing trousers is just as likely to be a female as one with long hair and wearing a dress. It is at this stage Kohlberg believes that the child begins to internalise their own gender identity.

Progress exercise

Explain the meaning of the terms used in Kohlberg's theory: gender labelling, gender stability and gender constancy.

## Evaluation

Kohlberg's theory of gender development emphasises the importance of the child's awareness of their own and other people's gender. The theory has generated lots of research into how a child acquires and actively uses this knowledge. A significant amount of research has provided evidence that children do indeed progress through the three stages of gender development, while other research has shown that the ages at which this occurs vary significantly (see Stagnor and Ruble 1987 for a review), Also there is a lot of debate about the importance of attaining gender constancy and therefore gender identity.

According to Kohlberg a child will identify with their own sex and engage in gender-appropriate behaviour only when they have reached the third stage of gender development (gender constancy). This is because, according to Kohlberg, they now understand that gender is constant and unchanging, and therefore a part of their static identity. However, Kohlberg's findings concerning the age at which gender constancy is reached were based on studies using pictures, where children were asked whether the gender identity of a girl or boy could change with alterations of clothing or hair length. Kohlberg found that it was only when children reached about 5 years of age that they were able to look beyond the surface changes shown in the pictures, and realise that gender identity remains the same. However more recent studies using a different approach have found that if children are asked direct questions about themselves, even 3 year olds know that they will remain the same gender when they grow up. Perhaps the pictures used in Kohlberg's study were seen by the children as representing something that was not linked to real life, and so unlike real life could be changed and manipulated at will.

### Evidence from other studies

Other studies such as Weinraub et al. (1984), have also revealed that 3 year olds are more able to label their own gender and to categorise pictures correctly if they have experienced playing with gender-type toys such as guns for boys and dolls for girls. So it seems that gender constancy can occur at an earlier age than Kohlberg theorised, if the child's environment is of a particular kind. However the causal role of early gender knowledge is still not totally clear. For example, a study by Perry, White and Perry (1984) found that boys' preferences for gender-type toys occurred earlier than their knowledge of gender stereotypes by approximately a year, whereas for girls the order was haphazard. For some girls preference for gender-type toys preceded gender knowledge, while for others the reverse was true. This seems to indicate that playing with gender-type toys does not always lead to an understanding of gender, or vice versa. The study mentioned earlier by Weinraub et al. (1984), investigated family characteristics to see if there was any link with parental attitudes and early gender role development, which would indicate a greater role played by social learning than by cognitive development. They found that fathers' attitudes and behaviours were closely related to their child's gender labelling. The more gender-type behaviour shown by the father, the stronger the child's gender-type toy preference (especially sons). In contrast, the attitude and behaviour of mothers had little effect on the gender labelling or toy preferences of the children. So it seems that the behaviour and attitudes of parents (especially the father) does have an effect on the child's development of gender identity, which is inconsistent with Kohlberg's cognitive theory.

## Gender schemas

If we consider what it means to be male or female in Western society today we may find ourselves thinking in terms of gender stereotypes as a way of differentiating between the sexes. For example, we may see females as nurturant, caring and sensitive, while males are aggressive, ambitious and dominant. Children are aware of these stereotypes from a young age and often select certain ones to incorporate into their own understanding of how males and females ought to behave. This set of ideas or stereotypes about each gender develops and changes as the child grows and learns, and is known as the child's **gender schema**. The content of an individual's schema continues to develop throughout childhood and beyond. Each of us has our own gender schema that we constantly refer to as we interpret our world and make decisions about our day-to-day lives.

## Gender schema theory

A key extension of Kohlberg's theory of gender development, known as gender schema theory, has been proposed by Carol Martin and Charles Halverson (1981, 1987). In agreement with Kohlberg, they believe that children become aware of their gender as they mature, and are motivated to acquire beliefs, interests and behaviours in line with the gender they relate to. But unlike Kohlberg they propose that this developing gender awareness begins as soon as the child begins *gender labelling* around age 2–3 (the first stage of Kohlberg's theory), so that sex-typed behaviours are clearly visible well before Kohlberg's final stage of *gender constancy*. According to Martin and Halverson, this early gender identity is achieved through the child actively incorporating information about the different genders into **gender schemas** that they can then act on. Initially, the child acquires a simple **ingroup/outgroup** schema that allows them to separate the behaviours/ roles of males and females. They then construct an own-sex schema that consists of plans of actions needed to perform various gender-consistent behaviours that will allow them to enact their own sex role. Once formed these gender schemas act as scripts for processing incoming social information. For example, any information that deviates from their gender-related knowledge (such as girls like to play with guns) is likely to be ignored, while information that is consistent with their gender related knowledge (such as girls like to play with dolls) is integrated into their existing gender schemas.

The process of rejecting or accepting specific gender information has been illustrated by Martin and Halverson (1983) in a study of children aged between 5–6 years. The children were exposed to a set of sixteen pictures, half of which showed a child actor performing gender-consistent activities (e.g. a boy playing with a lorry), and half of which showed a child actor performing gender-inconsistent behaviours (e.g. a girl chopping wood). One week later the children were tested to see what they could remember about the pictures. It was found that when the pictures portrayed gender-consistent behaviours, the children could easily remember the sex of the actor. However, when the actor's behaviour was gender inconsistent, the child's memory of it was often distorted and they would remember the sex of the actor as being gender consistent with the activity being performed. This study appears to indicate that children do indeed have strong tendencies to incorporate gender-consistent behaviours into their existing schemas, while ignoring behaviours that are gender inconsistent.

## Conclusion

Overall, Martin and Halverson's theory provides further understanding of the sex-typing process, and indicates how gender schemas may contribute to strong sex role preferences and behaviours long before the child reaches the stage where they understand that gender is a constant and unchanging part of our identity.

Generally, cognitive approaches have proved valuable in highlighting the active part children play in the acquisition of a gender identity. The theories have shown that children are not passive recipients of all they see and experience, but actively select and internalise behaviours that they can relate to and make sense of. However these approaches ignore the impact of culture and the environment on the child, and they also fail to look at why male and female gender roles are constructed and valued differently. Social learning theory and cross-cultural research can add to the findings of cognitive approaches, and should be part of an inclusive analysis. Only by pooling the findings of each approach will a more comprehensive understanding be reached of how and why males and females develop gender identities.

Progress exercise

1 Define the term gender schema.

2 Make a list of gender schemas that you have incorporated into your own beliefs about the roles of males and females.

## Summary

In this chapter we have discussed cognitive development theories of gender including Kohlberg's gender development theory and Martin and Halverson's gender schema theory. We have examined in detail the three stages of Kohlberg's theory: gender labelling, gender stability and gender constancy, and have evaluated the validity of the assumptions made. We have concluded that the age at which children acquire an understanding of gender, and begin to categorise others on the basis of this understanding, differs from child to child. We have also seen that the environment of the child has an impact on their understanding of gender. Martin and Halverson's gender schema theory has provided further evidence of the effect society has on the types of gender role behaviours internalised by the child, and their subsequent gender identity. Gender schema theory also illustrates how children begin to acquire gender knowledge at a much earlier age than postulated by Kohlberg. Overall, we have seen that cognitive approaches have proved most valuable in highlighting the active part children play in the acquisition of a gender identity.

## Further reading

Fagot, B.I. and Leinbach, M.D. (1989) The young child's gender schema: environmental input, internal organization. *Child Development* 60, 663–672. An interesting discussion on the effects of both social and cognitive factors in gender schema development.

Weisner, T.S. and Wilson-Mitchell, J.E. (1990) Nonconventional family lifestyles and sex-typing in six year olds. *Child Development* 61, 1915–1933. This detailed study provides an alternative view of the impact of the child's environment on their gender development.

# 8

# An alternative view
# of gender identity

Psychological androgyny
Bem's gender schema theory
Evaluation
Conclusion
Summary

### Psychological androgyny

So far we have seen that gender identity can be viewed as a sense of self, predisposed by biological influences and eventually gained through a process of social interaction. However, the traditional assumption of a *fixed* gender that is either masculine or feminine may not be adequate to describe all individuals.

Until recently the behaviours and identities of males and females have been constructed as opposites. Males are often seen as ambitious and oriented towards goal achievement in the world of work or sport, while females are depicted as caring and oriented towards the family and nurturing the young. There was no cross-over between the characteristics for each gender, as the way the gender identities were constructed meant that if a person was identified as having feminine qualities they could not also have male qualities. This idea of people being one or the other in terms of gender identity fits with the prevailing Western culture, which acts to separate and construct the roles and therefore identities of males and of females very differently.

The trouble is that some people perceive themselves as *both* masculine and feminine, while others do not feel as if they are either.

This problem has been investigated by Sandra Bem (1974), who has put forward the idea of a third gender identity, which she describes as **psychological androgyny**. This refers to cases where a sense of masculinity and femininity coexist within the same person. Bem believed that existing measures of gender identity were inadequate. She felt a more realistic approach would be to represent gender identity on an **orthogonal scale** rather than on a **continuum** as was traditional, e.g. Gough (1952), Strong (1943) (see Figure 8.1). She went on to develop the Bem Sex Role Inventory (BSRI), a questionnaire that could tease out aspects of masculine and feminine identities. An individual who completed the test would gain a score for both masculinity (which could be + or –) and a score for femininity (which again could be + or –). From these scores, Bem was able to identify individuals who perceived themselves as having both identities, i.e. who were psychologically androgynous, as well as individuals who perceived themselves as being neither masculine or feminine, i.e. were undifferentiated in gender terms.

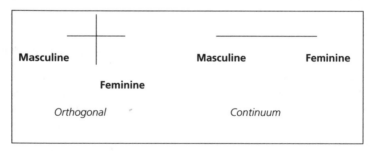

**Figure 8.1** Masculinity/femininity represented on an orthogonal scale and on a continuum

Review exercise

1   How does a continuum scale differ from an orthogonal scale?

2   Explain the meaning of psychological androgyny.

### Comparisons with sexual identity

Linked to the traditional dualistic interpretation of gender identity whereby an individual can only be either masculine or feminine (not both), is a similar construction of human sexuality. This has been criticised by Money (1987) who notes that sexuality (like gender identity) has been categorised as a dichotomy. For example, people are seen as either one thing or another (either gay or straight), when in reality several different patterns of human sexuality are possible, including heterosexuality, homosexuality and bisexuality. Money argues that this view of sexuality acts to narrow the human condition and places constraints on natural patterns of social behaviour. In a similar way Bem argues that the traditional view of gender identity could do the same. She proposes that the rigid sex role differentiation of masculinity and femininity, that is still very much a part of Western society, has outlived its usefulness. According to Bem it is better for people to define themselves in ways that allow them to behave in ways appropriate to the situations they find themselves in, rather than being constrained by culturally prescribed gender-appropriate behaviours. Therefore, Bem proposes that an androgynous society is psychologically healthier than a rigid sex-typed society.

Think of a social situation (e.g. a shopping trip) and using the headings: sex-typed masculine and sex-typed feminine, make a list underneath each one, of the stereotypical behaviours you think a person would show during the situation. Do you think an androgynous person might behave differently? Note down any differences.

Progress exercise

### BSRI categories

There are in fact eight sex role categories that are standard within the BSRI, (four female, four male) and an individual may score as one of them (see Table 8.1 next page). A problem with the scale, highlighted in a classic study by Broverman, Vogel, Broverman, Clarkson and Rosenkrantz (1972), is that individuals place a higher value on male characteristics, and see these as generally more indicative of health, than female characteristics.

Further evidence of a bias towards 'masculine' qualities is provided in a study by Dimitrovsky, Singer and Yinon (1989). They administered the BSRI to a sample of 200 male and 299 female soldiers, afterwards dividing them into the eight standard categories (see Table 8.1).

**Table 8.1** Percentages of Dimitrovsky et al.'s sample categorised as various sex role types

| Sex Type | Description | |
|---|---|---|
| Sex-typed males | Men scoring high on masculinity and low on femininity. | 41% |
| Sex-typed females | Women scoring high on femininity and low on masculinity. | 35% |
| Androgynous males | Men who score high on both masculinity and femininity. | 21% |
| Androgynous females | Women who score high on both masculinity and femininity. | 27% |
| Cross-sex-typed males | Men who score high on femininity and low on masculinity. | 11% |
| Cross-sex-typed females | Women who score high on masculinity and low on femininity. | 17% |
| Undifferentiated males | Men who score low on both masculinity and femininity. | 27% |
| Undifferentiated females | Women who score low on both masculinity and femininity. | 21% |

Dimitrovsky, Singer and Yinon then evaluated how well individuals in each category performed according to their own, peer and officer ratings of their effectiveness in training. From this they concluded that for both genders, 'superior adjustment is associated with instrumental masculine qualities'. In other words, those males categorised as either sex-typed masculine or androgynous, and females categorised as cross-sex-typed or androgynous, performed better overall than those in the other categories. This provides a clear demonstration of bias towards masculine qualities.

## Bem's gender schema theory

Common-sense tells us that people have different cognitive schemas for organising their understanding of themselves and others. However, Bem's theory (1981) proposes that these differences can be divided into just two categories: **gender schematic** and **gender nonschematic**. According to Bem some people are gender schematic in that they organise and understand things in their world according to gender categories, while others are gender nonschematic whereby gender is not relevant to that individual's understanding of themselves or others. For example, a gender schematic person would assume that males and females have very different roles in society, perhaps drawing on the belief that females are caring and sensitive, while males are tough and active. On the other hand a person who is gender nonschematic would consider that any role is appropriate for either gender. Of the eight categories on Bem's Sex Role Inventory (BSRI), it is the people who score as sex-typed that are considered to be gender schematic.

Write a list of the eight categories that make up Bem's sex role inventory and note which of them would be considered gender schematic.

Progress exercise

## Evaluation

If Bem's theory is correct, and gender schematic people do process and organise information in a way that differentiates between the genders, we would expect them to be more aware of gender-relevant material than gender nonschematics. We would also anticipate that because of their greater awareness of gender-relevant material, gender schematics would show more attention and more recall of such material.

### Research by Frable and Bem

A study by Frable and Bem (1985) attempted to show that an individual's perception of others in terms of gender categories is influenced by their gender schema. A group of students (ninety-six male, ninety-six female) were given the BSRI to complete, and subsequently divided into the eight categories that form the standard scoring framework. Those students who scored as sex-typed were considered to be gender schematic, while those who scored as androgynous were seen as gender nonschematic. All participants were then required to listen to a taped discussion in which six people talked about various aspects of college life, such as accommodation, food etc. while viewing photographs of the speakers. They were later required to match the photographs with written snatches of conversation taken from the discussion.

As well as gender, the researchers had also decided to look at the effect of race on the perception of the participants, and so had divided them into two groups. One of the groups was shown pictures of six males – three black, three white – and six females – three black, three white – to check the effect of race on the perception of the participant, while the other group was shown pictures of six white people – three men, three women – and six black people – three men, three women – to check the effect of gender on perception (see Table 8.2).

Frable and Bem's hypothesis for the study was that the gender schematic group should be more able to match the correct speech

| Table 8.2 Frable and Bem's gender/race condition | |
|---|---|
| Group 1 – to test the effect of race | Group 2 – to test the effect of gender |
| Shown pictures of: | Shown pictures of: |
| Six males (3 black + 3 white) | Six whites (3 male + 3 female) |
| Six females (3 black + 3 white) | Six blacks (3 male + 3 female) |

sample with the correct gender speaker more often than the gender nonschematic group. This is because if Bem's theory is correct the gender schematic group should be more aware of gender and so should be better able to recall who said what. In terms of race both groups should achieve similar results.

### Frable and Bem's findings

The findings of this study were that in the race condition no significant differences were found, both groups were similar in their perception of who said what. However, in the gender condition gender schematic participants were significantly more likely to match the correct statement with the correct sex, especially if the speaker was of the opposite sex to themselves. Frable and Bem concluded that this shows gender schematic participants were more in tune with the sex of the speaker (albeit of the opposite sex) than gender nonschematic participants, and were more likely to categorise speakers in terms of their gender.

A further study by Frable (1989) examined the effects of gender schema on stereotyping. Participants watched a video of a mock job interview for a position in management. They were presented with two excellent candidates (one male, one female), and two average candidates (one male, one female). Frable expected that if Bem's theory was correct the gender schematic individuals should devalue the female candidates, and judge the male candidates as more suitable for the job (as gender stereotyping would predict a male to be more suitable for a job in management than a female). This was found to be the case, and again highlights the effects on the behaviour of individuals who (according to the theory) are gender schematic.

### Conclusion

Overall, the two studies examined have provided evidence that Bem's gender schema theory is valid and does go some way to explain how individual schemas are organised in terms of gender. Some people do appear to judge and categorise others and themselves in terms of their gender and gender-appropriate behaviours etc., while others are more flexible and tend to ignore gender as a way of categorising behaviour. More research is needed to illuminate the wider effects of these two types of perception, gender schematic and gender nonschematic, and whether being androgynous (gender nonschematic) is a psychologically healthier way to be. Also the bias towards masculine qualities needs to be addressed, if a psychologically healthier society is ever to be achieved.

## Summary

The main focus of this chapter is to explore the issue that the traditional assumption of a *fixed* gender (one can only be *either* masculine *or* feminine) is inadequate to describe all individuals. A parallel is drawn with the problems of a fixed sexuality that allows only homosexuality or heterosexuality, and the point raised that other sexual orientations exist. The idea of psychological androgyny put forward by Sandra Bem (whereby males and females can have gender identities that incorporate both masculine and feminine qualities) is discussed as an alternative to the traditional approach. As well as this the Bem Sex Role Inventory (BSRI) is described whereby a individual's level of androgyny or sex typing can be measured. Lastly, Bem's gender schema theory, which purports that some people are gender schematic in that they think in terms of gender roles/stereotypes, or gender nonschematic whereby gender has no importance in their ways of making sense of the world, is discussed. Bem's belief that an androgynous society is psychologically healthier than a sex-typed society is raised but remains a question for further research.

## Further Reading

Weeks, J. (1986) *Sexuality*, London: Routledge. An interesting read for those interested in the many factors that make up our sexuality, both social and biological.

Bem, S.L. (1982) Gender schema theory and self-schema theory compared: a comment on Markus, Crane, Bernstein and Siladi's 'self-schemas and gender'. *Journal of Personality and Social Psychology* 43, 1192–94. A detailed examination and evaluation of Bem's work.

# Section III

## ADOLESCENCE

# 9

# The concept of adolescence

- Definition of adolescence
- Physical development
- Adolescent sexuality
- The search for identity
- Psychological turmoil?
- Correlates of stress during adolescence
- The timing of puberty
- Coleman's focal theory
- Evaluation
- Summary

## Definition of adolescence

As a child grows into adolescence, great changes take place in that child's life, physically, psychologically and socially. The move away from childhood and into adulthood brings with it responsibilities and choices not available to a child.

The term 'adolescent' comes from the Latin *adolescere* and literally means 'to grow into maturity', and the move from childhood to adulthood is marked by an extended period of growth. During this time the individual matures sexually, a period known as **puberty**, and becomes capable of reproduction. Also, cognitive changes take place, along with changes in interpersonal relationships, emotions and self-identity.

## Physical development

The age at which a young person reaches puberty varies, but normally occurs somewhere between the ages of 12 to 15 years in males, and 11 to 14 years in females. At the base of the brain lies the **pituitary gland**. At the onset of puberty this gland begins to secrete hormones, and to trigger the release of other hormones from various other glands. In males, these hormones act to stimulate the secretion of sex hormones (i.e. testosterone) in the testes, causing the production of sperm cells. This eventually leads to the first ejaculation of sperm from the penis, known as **spermarche**. In females the ovaries are stimulated to produce hormones (i.e. estrogen) that are responsible for the process of ovulation, leading to the release of ova (eggs). This is signified by the appearance of the first menstrual period or **menarche** as it is sometimes called (Hetherington and Parke 1999).

### Cross-cultural differences in the onset of menarche

For some women, the appearance of menarche is the true beginning of puberty (Brooks-Gunn and Ruble 1984). Cross-culturally the age that menarche occurs can vary widely. For example, Herman-Giddens et al. (1997) found that the onset of menarche for African-American females is typically around the age of 8–9 years. Other researchers have found that in underdeveloped countries such as New Guinea, a common age for the beginning of menarche is 17–18 years (Malcolm 1970). See Figure 9.1 for a visual comparison.

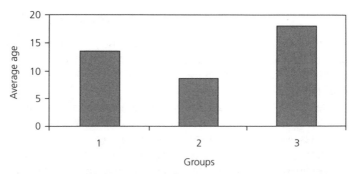

*Figure 9.1* **Comparison between different cultures of the average age at which menarche begins**

*Note:* Group 1 = Western, Group 2 = African/American, Group 3 = New Guinea

Although the average age at the onset of menarche between cultures appears to vary quite considerably, other research indicates that generally the age at the onset of menarche is declining. For example, Roche (1979) found that over the course of a century the age of first menstruation in Scandinavian countries dropped from 17 years in 1840, to 13 years in 1970. This appears to be a general trend in industrialized countries. We will discuss the various factors that may influence the onset of menarche later in this chapter.

### Primary sexual changes

In both sexes the adrenal glands are also stimulated and begin to produce other physical changes. These changes, along with the onset of menarche in females, and spermarche in males, are collectively known as **primary sexual changes**, because they are linked with the ability to reproduce. In females, these changes include an increase in the size of clitoris, vagina and uterus. In males, the enlargement of the penis and testes takes place, alongside the production of sperm (Tanner 1990).

### Secondary sexual changes

Other physical changes that take place during adolescence are known as **secondary sexual changes**, and these occur over a period of several years. For both sexes these changes include the development of pubic hair and changes in body shape. In males the voice deepens, muscles develop, and facial hair begins to grow, while in females the pelvis widens, breasts develop, and skin texture changes. Both sexes experience a rapid and substantial increase in height known as the 'growth spurt'. In males this begins a couple of years later than it does in females, but lasts longer (Tanner 1990).

1 Write a brief explanation of the physical changes that take place during adolescence for males and females (try to use the correct terminology).

2 Using Table 9.1 explain how various hormones also have an effect on the development of males and females.

Progress exercise

**Table 9.1** Major hormones involved in physical growth and development

| Gland | Hormone secreted | Function |
|-------|-----------------|----------|
| Pituitary | Growth hormones/Activating hormones | • Affects physical maturation<br>• Signals other glands to secrete |
| Ovaries (female) | Estrogen | • Release of egg (ova)<br>• Onset of menarche |
| Testes (male) | Testosterone | • Production of sperm cells<br>• Start of spermarche |
| Adrenal | Androgen | • Increase in size of clitoris, vagina and uterus<br>• Enlargement of penis and testes |

Source: Tanner (1990)

As discussed above, the age at the onset of menarche in industrialised countries seems to be declining. There are various factors that play a role in the timing of the onset of menarche, but traditionally the most influential is thought to be inheritance. Females whose mothers matured early tend to mature early themselves. However, environmental factors also play a part. For example, Moffitt, Caspi, Belsky and Silva (1992) found that family conflict and father absence from family life, was significantly correlated with early onset of menarche. This finding has been replicated by Wierson, Long and Forehand (1993), who demonstrated that divorce and marital conflict could be used to predict early onset. Environmental factors, such as choice of profession, also play a part in the timing of menarche. A study by Brooks-Gunn and

Warren (1985) found that occupations requiring high levels of activity, such as gymnastics or figure skating, can lead to a delay in the onset of menarche by up to one year. Other studies have looked at the parent-offspring relationship, and found the closer the relationship, the slower the onset of puberty (Steinberg 1987). This finding has also been reported in studies of primates (see Belsky et al. 1991). It seems that the timing of puberty can be tempered by both nature and nurture, and the task of researchers is to establish the extent of influence of the various factors.

### Adolescent sexuality

According to psychoanalytic theory, as discussed in Chapter 4, the beginning of puberty marks the end of the 'latency period' of psychosexual development – a time in which sexuality is forgotten – and the beginning of the 'genital period', where it reawakens. The genital stage is the last stage in Freud's theory of development, and culminates when the individual reaches sexual maturity. However, it appears that Freud may have been incorrect when he assumed children between the ages of 6 and 11 years have forgotten their early sexual curiosity. A study by Rosen and Hall (1984) has shown that sexual experimentation, for example masturbation, actually increases during this time. A survey by Elias and Gebhard (1969) found that more than half of boys and a third of girls aged between 4 and 14 years old, had engaged in some form of sexual play, such as manipulating the genitals of same-sex peers.

If sexuality continues to develop and grow throughout childhood, then how does it change during the period of adolescence? One finding is the importance that sexuality assumes once the individual reaches puberty. Up until that time children, although curious and experimenting with their sexuality, are still only playing. A child's sexuality is not yet part of their identity, whereas an adolescent must incorporate their sexuality as part of their self-concept. The need to express their sexuality (whatever it may be) becomes a vital need for the young person, in order to establish their identity.

In Western societies, heterosexuality is often regarded as the norm, and other sexual orientations seen as deviant. However, according to John Money (1987) sexual orientation is not something we can decide upon, but rather something that gradually happens to us. This means that the search for sexual identity can be a difficult journey for some individuals. The messages they receive through the media, through their families and peers, and even through sex education at school, depict heterosexuality as 'the natural order of things' (Money 1987).

Generally, sexuality is discussed much more openly in Western societies today than ever before. But rather than leading to a clearer understanding of the issues and arguments around sexuality, it appears that adolescents are becoming more and more confused. Dreyer (1982) notes that the idea of 'sex with affection' is an ambiguous one: should one truly love another person before participating in sexual intercourse, or is simply liking them enough? Young people receive mixed messages from parents and other sources. For example, parents may teach their offspring to value their sexuality and to avoid sexual encounters as a protection against unwanted pregnancies and/or sexually transmitted diseases, but at the same time encourage them to be popular and attractive. Television portrays those characteristics (popularity and attractiveness) alongside promiscuousness and sexual innuendo. Sexual participation is depicted through the media as a means to an end, a way of having a good time and being accepted into society. Gullotta, Adams and Alexander (1986) quote the definition of a virgin, according to one adolescent, as 'an awfully ugly third grader', in order to illustrate the social pressures facing young people to become sexually active. And on top of all this is the fear of not being 'normal' according to society, in terms of sexual orientation.

**Progress exercise**

Answer the following questions:

1 Name four factors that can have an effect on the early or late onset of menarche.

2 Explain why the search for sexual identity can be a difficult journey for some individuals.

3 Describe two mediums through which young people receive messages about sexual behaviour.

## The search for identity

Throughout childhood, children tend to see themselves in terms of physical attributes and personality characteristics. For example, a female child may view her identity as a girl with red hair and blue eyes, who is truthful and clever. A male child may see himself as a boy with blond hair and brown eyes, who is kind and funny. However, as these children reach puberty this perception changes, and the focus on the physical self shifts to a focus based on the kind of relationships they have with others. Now the individuals assesses themselves in terms of how they interact socially, for example whether they are expressive and outgoing, or shy and retiring, or whether they see themselves as dependable in a crisis etc. This perception of self, based on social actions, continues to evolve until in late adolescence the individual changes again, and now begins to identify themselves in terms of their political, social and/or philosophical views (Damon and Hart 1988).

As the young person strives to develop his or her identity the early perceptions of childhood, along with the newer perceptions of middle and late adolescence, play a part in shaping the emerging identity. In Chapter 10 the issue of identity is discussed in more detail along with Erikson's theory of lifespan development and Marcia's theory of identity.

## Psychological turmoil?

The bodily changes that take place throughout puberty, coupled with the move from childhood, where little or no responsibility and dependence on others is replaced with increasing amounts of responsibility and independence, can have a profound effect on the self-concept and behaviour of the individual.

According to G. Stanley Hall (1904) adolescence is a time of '*sturm und dieng*' or 'storm and stress', characterised by extreme mood swings and unpredictable behaviour. This traditional view is one shared by psychoanalytic theorists and in particular by Anna Freud (1969), who describes the young person as experiencing intense sexual feelings and excessive emotions caused by the growing intensity of inner drives.

However others, such as anthropologist Margaret Mead (1935), believe that the problems experienced by young people are caused by external pressures placed on the adolescent, rather than being the product of some inner turmoil. In Western society young people are faced with increasing independence from parents and figures of authority, along with changing relationships with their peers. They are also faced with major environmental changes such as going to college, leaving home to study at university, or starting a job, and must confront a wide range of competing values and ideals from parents, peers and the mass media providing them with choices and possible conflicts. These experiences, coupled with the heightened self-consciousness that accompanies adolescence, can serve to hamper the gradual move from childhood to adulthood.

## Correlates of stress during adolescence

### Self-perception

One interpersonal issue that may contribute to stress during adolescence is that of self-perception. Many young people who had previously been highly confident and outgoing suddenly become self-conscious. Appearance often becomes a major concern, as well as worries about weight, height and rate of development. A study by Brooks-Gunn and Warren (1988) found that in general females like to be perceived as attractive and therefore physical changes they experience that are in line with the 'feminine ideal' (i.e. those portrayed through the media etc.), are usually welcomed. For example, breasts are perceived as a positive thing, and females often feel better about themselves once they have developed in this area. Being too fat is a concern of many adolescent females, particularly in Western societies, and may lead to endless fad diets and exercise regimes. However, in some African cultures, plump females are seen as sexually attractive. A study by Helman (1990) found that some wealthy families in parts of West Africa actually send their daughters to fattening houses, where they are fed highly fattening food and given minimal exercise, to make them plump.

Males seem to worry less about their body image than females, and are more likely to welcome weight gain, according to a study by Richards, Boxer, Petersen and Albrecht (1990). It appears that most males wish to be tall, handsome and powerful, and if they do worry about aspects of body image, it is often to do with physical ability, rather than physical appearance (Berscheid et al. 1973). However, in terms of who they are attracted to, males place a higher value on physical attractiveness than females, who themselves are more concerned with the status and financial success of their partner (Feingold 1992).

So what is the effect of these changing perceptions of body image and possible worries about achievements and/or expectations for the future?

A study by Masterson (1967), which consisted of interviewing a large group of adolescents between the ages of 12 and 18 years old, found 65 per cent were suffering from some form of stress. However, a further study by Rutter (1976), compared the psychological health of 10 year olds, 14 year olds and adults, and found no significant differences between them. Furthermore, a significant number of the 14 year olds suffering from psychiatric problems, had experienced them since childhood. Several other studies have also concluded that adolescence is not necessarily a time of stress and emotional turmoil.

### *Self-harm*

More recent research has found that suicidal thoughts are shockingly common among adolescents and young adults (Dubow et al. 1989). Further evidence of this comes from a survey of high-school students by Smith and Crawford (1986), who found that approximately 63 per cent had considered suicide and almost 11 per cent had actually attempted it. This trend has continued to increase over the past thirty years and is now the third leading cause of death for this age group, behind only accidents and murder. Findings also indicate gender differences, in that females attempt suicide more often, but males are more successful. This appears to be true across the various cultures that have been studied (Girard 1993).

Is it possible to identify which young people are more likely to attempt suicide? Research indicates that those most at risk are often severely depressed, abusing drugs, or displaying some other type of psychological disorder (Garland and Zigler 1993). They have often experienced failure at school or college, or in their relationships outside the family, or they may be experiencing deteriorating relationships at home with parents or siblings. Other indicators can be a loss of interest in hobbies, and an inability to cope with day-to-day problems (Berman and Jones 1991).

## Eating disorders

If suicide is a major risk that most commonly affects young men, then eating disorders present a similar high risk to young women. The two most common eating disorders are **bulimia nervosa** and **anorexia nervosa** (see Table 9.2 for DSM-IV criteria). They are likely to occur anytime between the age of 10 and the early twenties. Young women with anorexia have an inexplicable fear of being fat and will do anything to avoid it, including starving themselves. They often lose 25 per cent of their body weight and become so weak and depleted that they have to be hospitalised and treated physically. Those anorexics who survive into adulthood, tend to retain their dissatisfaction with their bodies, and continue to diet on and off throughout their adult years (Heatherton et al. 1997).

Bulimia nervosa, like anorexia, is characterised by a fear of becoming fat. The difference is that in this case the young person (typically female), alternates between periods of binge eating followed by either self-induced vomiting or taking laxatives, to compensate for the amount of food eaten and prevent weight gain. Bulimics risk developing metabolic problems and other abnormalities such as the loss of stomach acid through frequent vomiting (American Psychiatric Association 1994). However, unlike anorexia, bulimia rarely leads to death, and intervention is much more likely to be successful.

What causes some adolescents to manifest illnesses such as anorexia or bulimia, but not others? One striking factor is that this type of disorder is notably more common in Western than non-Western societies (Cooper 1994), indicating a strong cultural component. The constant pressure on young Western women to maintain a thin body shape (perpetuated through the media) seems to be the obvious explanation for the common occurrence of eating disorders. In recent decades, the appearance of super-thin models like Twiggy, and the currently popular waif-like shape epitomised by Kate Moss, has meant that these social pressures have escalated. Coincidently, so has the occurrence of eating disorders. A survey of American beauty contestants found that more than half of them were 85 per cent or less than their expected body weight (Barlow and Durand 1995), which is actually one of the DSM-IV criteria for anorexia nervosa. However, although social pressures appear to play a major role in the occurrence of eating disorders, they aren't the only explanation. Not every adolescent exposed to social pressures to be

**Table 9.2** DSM-IV criteria for bulimia and anorexia nervosa

| Bulimia nervosa | Anorexia nervosa |
| --- | --- |
| • Numerous episodes of binge eating, in which more food is eaten in a two-hour period than most people would consume, and the eater experiences a lack of control over his or her eating behaviour. | • The individual has a body weight that is less than 85% of that expected.<br><br>• There is an intense fear of becoming fat in spite of being considerably underweight. |
| • There is frequent, inappropriate compensatory behaviour to prevent weight from being gained; examples include self-induced vomiting, excessive exercise, going without meals, and misuse of laxatives. | • The individual's thinking about his or her weight is distorted, either by exaggerating its importance to self-evaluation or by minimising the dangers of being considerably underweight. |
| • The above occurs at a rate of twice a week or more over a period of three months. | • In females, the absence of three or more consecutive menstrual cycles, known as amenorrhoea. |
| • The individual's self-evaluation depends excessively on his or her shape and weight. | |

thin, develops an eating disorder. In fact the majority do not. It seems that other factors predispose some individuals to be vulnerable to this type of social pressure. One of these factors is thought to be **clinical depression**, and lots of research has provided evidence of this (see Ben-Tovim and Crisp 1979; Piran et al. 1985). Other research by Benokraitis (1996) has found that most young people who suffer from these diseases are from families of fairly high **socioeconomic status**. Anorexics often come from high-achieving families, where the mother is domineering and over-protective, and the father stays very much in the background emotionally (Carson and Butcher 1992). It seems there are many factors that play a part in perpetuating these harrowing illnesses, and the cure is likely to prove both complex and challenging.

## The timing of puberty

Whether puberty begins early or late can have some lasting effects on the psychological development of males, whereas there seems to be little or no effect on females. Males who develop early have an advantage both physically (in sport etc.) and psychologically, in terms of the development of social skills and confidence in relationships with the opposite sex. A study by Clausen (1975) has shown that males who develop late are more likely to be more self-conscious and less socially adept than early developers, and these differences seem to persist into adulthood. Perhaps this is one of the root causes of the stress some theorists believe adolescents suffer from.

Review exercise

Draw up a table showing the factors that affect the physical and psychological development of adolescents in the following areas: puberty, sexuality, self-perception and self-harm.

## Coleman's focal theory

In agreement with the view that adolescence is a time of change, but not necessarily a time of 'storm and stress', Coleman (1974) argues that most adolescents can cope with changes or difficulties that may occur in their lives, as they have the ability to focus on each new problem as it arises. This idea of focusing on a problem in order to overcome it became known as focal theory, and evidence to support it comes from a large-scale study of 800 boys and girls aged between 11 and 17 years. Coleman and Hendry (1990) conducted interviews on these young people and asked them to discuss subjects they found stressful, such a self-image, career choices, peer, sexual and parental relationships. They found that each issue seemed to have a different distribution curve, reaching a high level or peak of importance at a different age (see Figure 9.2). For example, worries about peer relationships peaked at an earlier age than occupational choice. There were also individual differences in the ages at which adolescents experienced these problems.

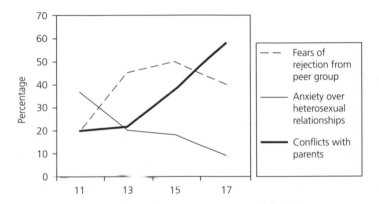

*Figure 9.2* **Issues reaching peaks of importance at different ages (Coleman and Hendry 1990)**

## Evaluation

It appears that adolescence is a time of social and physical change, but not a constant battle of storm and stress as traditionally thought. While Mead has highlighted the external social pressures, Coleman and Hendry's research has shown that instability or change occurs at different times in an adolescent's life and can be successfully negotiated by the majority of young people. These findings have been replicated in a study by Kroger (1985) carried out on large samples of young people from North America and New Zealand. Other researchers (e.g. Simmonds and Blyth 1987), have found, in agreement with Coleman's theory, that those adolescents who do experience extreme stress are likely to be facing more than one interpersonal issue at a time. Overall, Coleman's focal theory has been widely accepted as an important contributor to our understanding of adolescence.

Describe Coleman's focal theory and give one piece of evidence to support it.

## Summary

In this chapter we have discussed the development of the adolescent through puberty, self-perception and sexuality. We have seen how physical growth evolves along with psychological development. We have also considered the various factors that can have an effect on the timing and rate of development, including cultural factors and individual differences. We have discussed in depth whether adolescence is a time of great stress and turmoil, as traditional theorists often thought, and have concluded that although some young people may feel more or less stress at particular times, overall the stress experienced is no more than that felt at other times during the life cycle. A theory that is discussed and seems to provide evidence that young people can cope adequately is Coleman's focal theory. Coleman believes that the reason young people are able to cope with external stressors, rather than experiencing them as extreme turmoil, is because they normally only experience them one at a time, and so are able to deal with each problem as it arises. Finally, we have also discussed some specific problems that can occur during this time, such as eating disorders and suicide, and have looked briefly at possible self-harm indicators.

## Further Reading

Attie, I. and Brooks-Gunn, J. (1989) Development of eating problems in adolescent girls: a longitudinal study. *Developmental Psychology* 25, 70–79. An interesting and informative study for those concerned about eating disorders.

Foucault, M. (1984) *The History of Sexuality: An Introduction*, Harmondsworth: Penguin. A rather difficult read, but informative for students wishing to explore further the ways that sexuality has been depicted historically.

McClintock, M.K. and Herdt, G. (1996) Rethinking puberty: the development of sexual attraction. *Current Directions in Psychological Science* 5, 178–183. A clear and detailed discussion on the factors that contribute to the development of sexual attraction.

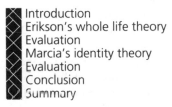

# 10

# Theories of adolescence

## Introduction

Erik Erikson's first teaching post in America was at Harvard Medical School in Boston, where he spent many years cultivating the view that personality could develop from an interaction of the self and society. After a spell at Yale University, he was offered a position at the University of California, and it was during this time that he carried out his famous studies of modern life among native Americans, such as the Sioux and the Yurok. In 1950 Erikson wrote his first book *Childhood and Society*, which contained summaries of his studies of native Americans, a basic outline of his version of Freudian theory, along with analyses of Adolf Hitler, Maxim Gorky, Martin Luther King and Mahatma Ghandi. Erikson never actually met these four historical figures, but analysed each of them from afar. He also included a discussion of the 'American personality'. Books he has written since have followed similar topics, but it was for his work refining and expanding Freud's stage theory of development into his own whole life theory, that he became most famous. In writing this theory Erikson drew on his past experiences and observations, but his ideas on adolescence came mainly from his observations of emotionally disturbed young people receiving therapy.

## Erikson's whole life theory

Eric Erikson was a practising psychoanalyst, and therefore accepted Freud's ideas concerning unconscious instincts and motivations, as basically true. He agreed with the basic premise of the **Oedipal complex**, whereby the child must overcome his/her attachment to the opposite sex parent and identify with the parent of the same sex, but felt that social and cultural influences also played an active role in shaping personality. Erikson (1950) put forward his own idea of a theory of development that expanded Freud's psychosexual stages into a whole life theory. He called his stages **psychosocial** to highlight the interaction of psychological and social factors, and argued that they are applicable to all people, from all cultures.

Erikson believed that personality operates by the **epigenetic principle**, which means the development of personality follows a *predetermined order* of stages. Each stage must be negotiated before the individual progresses to the next stage. Erikson assumes each of us goes through a series of eight developmental stages, each of which involve a **crisis** that we must negotiate and resolve within an optimal time period. Of the eight stages put forward by Erikson, only stage five is relevant to adolescence, therefore this stage will be discussed in the most detail. The crisis that faces the adolescent and must be resolved during this stage, is that of identity.

The way we negotiate and resolve each crisis has an effect on our future development that can be either positive or negative. In order to achieve a positive outcome the person must attain a balance between the two opposing attitudes that form the crisis. If the person develops more towards one attitude than the other, for example they mistrust the world more than they trust it, then they risk developing **maladjusted tendencies** or worse still **malignant tendencies**.

Explain the meaning of the following terms used by Erikson: epigenetic principle, crisis, psychosocial.

### Stage one: trust versus mistrust

The first psychosocial stage is called 'trust versus mistrust' and occurs in the first year of life. The child must learn to trust others, but without completely eliminating the capacity to mistrust. If a balance between trust and mistrust is achieved, the child will develop the virtue of **hope**.

### Stage two: autonomy versus shame and doubt

This stage occurs around the second and third year of life, and incorporates the anal-muscular stage of development. Parents must allow their child to explore the environment, in order that he or she begins to develop a sense of independence and **autonomy**. If the child achieves a balance between autonomy, and shame and doubt, then they will develop the virtue of willpower, which will equip them with the determination to succeed in the face of difficulties.

### Stage three: initiative versus guilt

Around the age of 4 to 5 years Erikson believes children enter the genital-locomotor stage, where they are faced with a crisis between believing in themselves enough to take the initiative, in terms of trying out new things, or becoming inhibited through feelings of self-doubt and guilt.

Erikson includes the Freudian experience of the **Oedipal complex** in this stage, believing that the child's reluctance to relinquish their closeness with the opposite sex parent must be dealt with very sensitively, if the child is to avoid feeling guilty about their feelings towards that parent.

If the child develops a balance between initiative and guilt, they will evolve the virtue of purpose. This will enable them to pursue their own goals with determination, but with a sense of respect for others, and a sense of moral obligation.

## Stage four: industry versus inferiority

Children enter this stage at about 6 years old and continue until they are about 12. During this time the child must develop the capacity for industry by learning how things work and the various materials things can be made from. Peers also begin to play an increasingly important role in the child's development, especially in terms of their **self-esteem**. The correct balance between industry and inferiority leads to the virtue of competency, whereby the person believes in their abilities and so will try their hand at many different things, and won't give up if they fail first time.

## Stage five: identity versus role confusion

This stage begins around puberty and continues until the person reaches 18 to 20 years old. The main task for the individual is to achieve a sense of their own identity and avoid role confusion. In order to understand how this may occur it is important to review Erikson's basic belief about human development. Erikson believes that throughout life people evolve simultaneously in three ways: biologically, socially and psychologically.

During adolescence young people experience developmental changes that have a profound effect on how they feel about their bodies. Not only are these changes physical in nature, so that the young person must almost *relearn* how to feel comfortable and at ease with their body. They also concern the young person's sexuality, including their sexual preferences, orientation and ultimately their identity as a fully-evolved sexual adult. The need to find a place in society is part of this development, and societies that provide clear **rites of passage**, such as traditional rituals or accomplishments that help distinguish the adult from the child, go some way to help ease the journey. In this way the irresponsible but powerless time of childhood is gradually set aside, while the responsible and more powerful time of adulthood is taken on.

*Identity crisis*

According to Erikson, young people need to know who they are and what they want out of life before they can move on to the formation of a stable adult identity. He states that 'adolescence is not an affliction, but a normative crisis, i.e. a normal phase of increased conflict'.

Erikson (1968) believes that this increased conflict experienced by adolescents and which comes about from uncertainty about their identity, or identity diffusion, has four major components:

1 *Intimacy*: a fear of commitment to others as it may involve loss of identity.
2 *Diffusion of time*: a disbelief in the possibility that time may bring change, yet a fear that it might.
3 *Diffusion of industry*: a lack of concentration or too much focus on a particular activity.
4 *Negative identity*: a scathing hostility towards the identity offered through one's family and community.

This view of increased conflict appears to agree with Hall's (1904) belief that adolescence is a time of 'storm and stress' (see Chapter 9). However, Erikson (unlike Hall) doesn't just describe the crisis but attempts to find ways of overcoming it. If the evolving person is unsure of their place in society, which Erikson believes most adolescents are, then they risk developing role confusion, which Erikson (1968) describes as an **identity crisis**. He believes that one way of resolving this crisis is for the adolescent to take some time out, perhaps to go off on their own, and to get to know who they are and what they want in life. He talks about the idea of **psychosocial moratorium**, which simply means to delay the onset of adulthood. In many Western societies young people are encouraged to go travelling, or to take a temporary job before committing themselves to more permanent life choices. In this way the individual gains more time and insight into what they really want out of life, and the choices available to them. If they make their life choices too soon, a situation Erikson calls **premature foreclosure**, they risk an identity crisis in later life.

A complication in this stage of development can occur if the person becomes so involved in a particular role in society, that they lose tolerance for anything else. An example of this is when a young person joins a religious cult and takes on the beliefs and behaviours of the cult to such an extent that their previous views are forgotten. Erikson call this maladaptive tendency **fanaticism**.

However, Erikson describes a further problem in this stage that may be even harder to deal with than fanaticism, which he calls the malignant tendency of **repudiation**. This is where the adolescent withdraws from the adult world, and casts aside any thoughts of achieving an identity. He or she may become involved in destructive activities that could include taking harmful drugs or excesses of alcohol, or they may simply withdraw from society and live in a world of psychotic fantasy.

If a balance is achieved between identity and role confusion, then the individual will attain the virtue of fidelity. Erikson uses this term to mean that a person has found their place in society, and can accept and live by the standards set by that society. They may want to change some things about the society in which they live, but they will go about it in a way that is acceptable and humane.

### Stage six: intimacy versus isolation

This is the first stage of young adulthood and occurs around the age of 18 years and extends until the person is around 30. Here the individual must achieve a balance between intimacy and isolation. Presuming the person has achieved the earlier stage and feels comfortable with their own identity and their place in society the next step is to find someone or some others to share it with. Intimacy is the ability to feel close to others, whether as a friend or lover, without fear of losing your own sense of self.

Those who achieve a balance between isolation and intimacy are said to have developed the virtue of love. In the context of Erikson's theory, love means accepting other people for all their faults and differences, and retaining a mutual devotion. This devotion includes not only the love for a life partner, but also for friends, colleagues and neighbours.

### Stage seven: generativity versus stagnation

This is the stage of middle adulthood, and often includes the period when parents are involved in raising their children. Generally in Western societies this occurs from the mid twenties and continues up until the mid-fifties. **Generativity** is an extension of the love acquired in the previous stage and is the concern we feel for future generations and humanity as a whole. Erikson believes that we practise generativity not only through having children, but also through social activism, through teaching, writing, the arts and sciences.

Achieving a balance between stagnation and generativity leads to the virtue of caring, and provides a bedrock for the person throughout the rest of his/her life.

### Stage eight: ego integrity versus despair

This is the last of Erikson's stages of development, and by now the individual has reached late adulthood. At this time people often find themselves in a similar position as when they were just starting out as a young adult. They have time on their hands, their children have grown up and left home, and they may have retired from their job. The successful negotiation of this final stage results in the person developing wisdom. This means that they approach death without fear, and so are able to give to children the ultimate gift of life. To quote from Erikson (1950), 'healthy children will not fear life if their elders have integrity enough not to fear death'. This is true wisdom.

1 Describe in detail Erikson's fifth stage of development, and discuss the problems facing an adolescent during this stage.

Review exercise

### Evaluation

Erikson is one of the main advocates for the stage approach to personality development. Most other personality theorists are opposed to this, preferring instead a gradual approach where individuals pass through phases or transitions. In terms of real life it becomes hard to defend Erikson's view of stages, especially because of his belief that there are **optimal time periods** within which each stage must be resolved. Behaviour across cultures often differs markedly, for example

| Table 10.1 Summary of Erikson's whole life theory plus Freud's psychosexual stages | | | | |
|---|---|---|---|---|
| Stage | Age | Crisis | Virtue | Freud's psychosexual stage |
| 1 | 0–1 | Trust vs mistrust | Hope | Oral |
| 2 | 1–3 | Autonomy vs shame and doubt | Willpower | Anal |
| 3 | 3–6 | Initiative vs guilt | Purpose | Phallic |
| 4 | 6–12 | Industry vs inferiority | Competence | Latency |
| 5 | 12–18 | Identity vs role confusion | Fidelity | Genital |
| 6 | 20s–30s | Intimacy vs isolation | Love | |
| 7 | 30s–50s | Generativity vs stagnation | Care | |
| 8 | 50s and beyond | Ego integrity vs despair | Wisdom | |

in some cultures young people are married by the time they are 15 years old, whereas in others they are still at school. In some cultures infants are fully weaned in the first year of life, whereas in others children of 5 years old are still being fed at the breast. Even the timing of motor development can vary between cultures (Harkness and Super 1995). Therefore, to propose optimal times for the resolution of specific stages of development, could undermine and devalue the experiences of many individuals from a variety of cultures.

Although Erikson observed other cultures while developing the ideas that eventually formed his theory of personality (e.g. the Yurok and Sioux Indians), he worked mainly in Europe and parts of the USA. Therefore his theory may still suffer from **ethnocentrism**, as it is derived mainly from Western cultures. His major innovation was to apply his whole life theory to major historical figures such as Martin

Luther King and Mahatma Ghandi (1969). He calls this method **psychohistory**, and has provided some interesting insights into the life experiences that helped shape these individuals. However, Erikson did not carry out any experimental studies to test his theory, and particularly concerning his ideas about adolescence, he relied mainly on observations of disturbed teenagers during therapy. This is obviously a biased sample, and his conclusions drawn from the behaviours observed cannot necessarily be applied to all young people.

A further criticism of Erikson's theory revolves around the issue of **generalisability**. Erikson claims that his theory of psychosocial stages applies equally to males and females, yet the theory is based on studies involving only males. This means that the male experience is being held up as the standard by which female experience is judged. This is a problem in many areas of research and illustrates the wider argument put forward by theorists such as Dale Spender (1983), who argue that women are often 'invisible' in our culture, due to knowledge being constructed from a male viewpoint.

Evidence that individuals do appear to progress through the stages of development put forward in Erikson's theory, comes from a study by Ryff and Heinke (1983). Three groups of adults took part in the study: young, middle-aged, and old-aged. Participants were asked to complete a number of personality questionnaires, two of which related to Erikson's concepts of generativity (during middle age) and integrity (during old age). They found that the groups perceived themselves as being most generativity-oriented at middle age, and as having higher integrity at old age.

### Research evidence concerning adolescence

Evidence to support Erikson's belief, that establishing an identity in adolescence is crucial for later successful relationships, comes from a **longitudinal** study by Kahn, Zimmerman, Csikszentmihalye and Getzels (1985). Students were assessed and given identity scores in 1963; the lower their score the less established the identity of the young person. Twenty years later the marital status of the individuals who took part was investigated. Females who had scored low in the original assessment, were more likely to be divorced or separated than those who had scored high, and a significant number of low-scoring males had never married and remained single.

One implication of Erikson's theory is that adolescents should suffer low self-esteem because of the stress and uncertainty they face as they negotiate and renegotiate who they are. However, a study by Marsh (1989) found that if changes in self-image do occur during adolescence they are more likely to be positive than negative. Also, if adolescents do suffer reduced self-esteem, then it is usually associated with several life changes occuring in a short space of time, such as starting a new school, or divorcing parents etc. (Simmons and Blyth 1987). Also these sorts of life events generally cause stress at any age, not just during adolescence.

## Marcia's identity theory

Inspired by the work of Erikson, and drawing on the findings of his own research, including detailed interviews with adolescents, Marcia (1967) put forward an alternative theory of adolescent identity, one that would facilitate empirical research. The central premise of this theory is that young people are faced with various choices and alternatives in life, before they finally make a commitment to a particular life course. This commitment, once made, will include the individual's sense of who they are, and where they are going. In other words they will have achieved a sense of identity.

### The four statuses

Marcia identified four statuses that identity can take, and individuals may only use one or may use all at different times. These are not stages but orientations, and are as follows:

1  *Identity diffusion*: this is where the individual has not thought too deeply about the issue of identity, and is not committed to any particular choices. Some see this as a state of conflict and confusion, as the young person is unable to formulate a clear self-definition and goal in life.

2  *Identity foreclosure*: this is where the adolescent has committed themselves to the roles and values prescribed by their parents, without any thought of possible alternatives. This may seem like a safe route to take, where anxieties and uncertainties are avoided, but may lead to problems in later life. Erikson also refers to this concept in stage five of his theory.

3 *Identity moratorium*: here the adolescent delays making any choices to do with their life course or personal identity, until they have had the chance to explore all options. Erikson also refers to this concept and sees it as a good way of developing a true sense of self.

4 *Identity achievement*: the individual has been through a crisis but has resolved it and emerged with strong commitments, goals and a clear sense of identity.

Unlike Erikson's theory, these four statuses are not stages, and therefore do not have to be negotiated in sequence. However, Marcia does believe that in order to attain identity achievement and so cope with adulthood, the individual must successfully complete identity moratorium.

## Evaluation

A review of several studies by Waterman (1982) found that of Marcia's four statuses, the two concerning diffusion and foreclosure were the most common during adolescence (i e 11–17 year olds). This implies that the theory has some credibility in terms of its application to young people. Also a study by Meilman (1979), found that among young males the statuses were related to age. For example, he found that younger males of 12–18 years were generally experiencing diffusion or foreclosure, and older males over 18 years were generally identity achievers. These same findings however *do not* apply to females, and Marcia admits that his theory can only be applied, with any reliability, to males.

Both Erikson (1968) and Marcia (1966) appear to assume that once an adolescent has achieved a stable sense of identity they are unlikely to lose it again. However, Marcia (1976) conducted follow-up interviews after his initial study and found that six years later some of the young people who had achieved a sense of identity had returned to the foreclosure or diffusion identity status. This possible feature of identity development is not addressed in either theory.

Although Marcia's theory is often said to be more realistic than Erikson's because it allows for a more flexible approach to identity achievement, it is also open to many of the same criticisms. These mainly revolve around a lack of empirical evidence. The interviews Marcia conducted cannot be used as reliable evidence for the following reasons: 1) they are a snapshot of real life; 2) they create **demand characteristics** in that the young people may only be saying what they think the interviewer wants to hear; 3) they consisted of only male participants and so cannot be generalised to females.

## Conclusion

Both Erikson's whole life theory and Marcia's identity theory put forward a framework of human development that can be used to understand the difficulties facing individuals, and in this case particularly adolescents, as they attempt to negotiate the journey from the cradle to the grave. Although Marcia is concerned *only* with the achievement of identity, his theory compliments and can be integrated into Erikson's whole life theory.

## Summary

In this chapter we have discussed Erikson's whole life theory of development, focusing in most detail on his ideas concerning the adolescent's achievement of identity during stage five, with examples of the various crises and experiences that must be resolved. Erikson's belief that we must pass through eight stages, all of which must be resolved successfully if we are to reach old age with any sense of happiness, raises the issue of people from different cultures reaching developmental landmarks at different times, and so casts some doubt on cross-cultural applications of the theory. Also, the lack of female participants in Erikson's early observations, raises the issue of generalisability. However, the theory does appear to be useful in providing some insight into the human condition. Studies have provided evidence that individuals do pass through at least some of the stages, at the relevant ages. Others have supported Erikson's belief that forming an identity in adolescence is crucial to later successful intimate relationships. In this chapter we have also reviewed Marcia's contribution to this area, and have seen how his theory compliments that of Erikson's. We have reviewed some evidence that supports Marcia's ideas, and some issues that refute it, such as the instability of identity even after it has been achieved. Lastly, we have briefly discussed the issue of lack of a solid empirical basis, which applies to both of these theories.

## Further reading

Erikson, E.H. (1950) *Identity: Youth and Crisis*, New York: Norton. This is structured like a collection of essays, and provides an excellent read for students studying personality as well as the general reader.

Marcia, J. (1966) Development and validation of ego identity status. *Journal of Personality and Social Psychology* 3, 551–558. An interesting and detailed account of Marcia's ideas.

# 11

# Other influences on development

## Introduction

So far in this section on adolescence, we have discussed the concept of adolescence and have examined the theories of Erikson and Marcia. We have focused principally on what it means to be an adolescent living in a Western culture, and have considered the various factors e.g. 'rites of passage', that may have an impact on the process of development, from child to adult.

In the first half of this final chapter on adolescence, we will consider the impact of parents and peers on the behaviour of the young person, and discuss cultural differences during adolescence. In the second half we will look at a specific life event that effects a significant number of young people: pregnancy. As well as discussing cross-cultural differences we will consider the various outcomes that pregnancy and being a young parent can create.

## Influence of peers on social behaviour

The *Oxford English Dictionary* defines a peer as *a person who is equal in ability, standing, rank, or value; a contemporary*. This can be compared with the view of developmental psychologists who define peers as social equals, or as individuals who *for the moment are operating at similar levels of behavioural complexity* (Lewis and Rosenblum 1975). Both definitions highlight the fact that age is not necessarily an important factor in determining who your peers are. More important is that levels of competence and areas of interest are similar.

A study by Hartup (1983) found that interaction between children of different ages can be crucial in terms of the development of particular social competencies. For example, older children interacting with younger ones are more likely to develop compassion and caregiving skills, as well as assertiveness and leadership skills. While younger children can acquire a variety of skills from watching older peers, including for example how to ask for help, and how to defer gracefully to the directions of older and more powerful associates. Same-age peers are much less critical and directive towards each other, and are more likely to try out new ideas together.

### Friends

During adolescence the nature of friendship for boys and girls changes in different ways. For girls, these changes mean that they begin to see their friends less as playmates and more as confidants who can provide social and emotional support (Urlberg et al. 1995). Girls often become involved in intense relationships at this time, and so are more likely to have one-to-one friendships with other girls, rather than forming into groups. Boys on the other hand, have less intense relationships, and are therefore more likely to form into groups. They become more focused on asserting their independence, and so generally prefer groups of friends who will act as allies.

As young people approach mid-adolescence, girls and boys begin to come together and form into small groups of close friends, known as **cliques** (Rubin et al. 1998). Cliques often develop distinct dress codes and language that sets them apart from other cliques, and gives members of the clique a sense of belonging. Sometimes different cliques come together and form into crowds of friends. The crowd then acts as a social facilitator, as members organise social activities together, such as parties, meeting up at clubs, or holidays etc. Sexuality also becomes important during this time, and many young people begin experimenting with sex. Being part of a clique enables young people to interact with members of the opposite sex in casual social situations, rather than having to be intimate straight away. Eventually cross-sex relationships begin to develop and the dynamics within the clique shift from individual friends to couples. Once couples form the clique begins to break down, having served its purpose in bringing males and females together.

### Do peers influence conformity?

How influential are these groups, or their individual members, in terms of **conformity** or non-conformity to moral, social or legal codes of behaviour? Research indicates that young people are highly influenced by their peer group. A study by Thomas Berndt (1979) found that as young people develop from late childhood into early adolescence, conformity to **pro-social behaviour** stays more or less the same. But, conformity to **anti-social behaviour** begins to increase, reaching a peak at approximately 15 years old and then declining throughout the rest of the adolescent period (see Figure 11.1). Perhaps conformity to peer groups is a prerequisite to achieving independence and autonomy as an adult. Steinberg and Silverberg (1986) argue that as the young person struggles to become independent from their parents, they use the security provided by the peer group and the self-confidence that comes with it, to take that final step towards independence.

### Relationship with parents during adolescence

As noted earlier, adolescence is often seen as a time of conflict and strife. Teenagers are thought to experience **cross-pressures** from parents and peers, whose values and behaviours differ considerably, causing the young person turmoil and stress. However, research has shown this is not always the case (see Chapter 9). Many young people make the transition from childhood to adulthood with relative ease, and very little in the way of stress. So where is the conflict that so many early researchers referred to? Research by Dishion, Patterson,

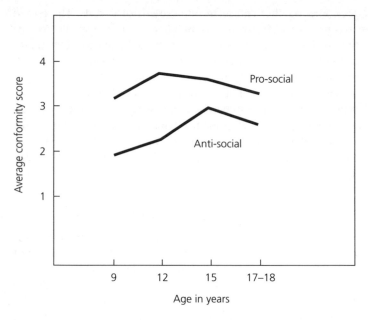

*Figure 11.1* **Pro-social and anti-social behaviour during adolescence**

Stoolmiller and Skinner (1991), has shown that problems can occur if the young person becomes involved with what we might call a **deviant peer group**, one which endorses anti-social behaviours such as criminal activities. These types of behaviours are likely to alienate parents, teachers and even other peers. Therefore, young people becoming involved in social groups of this kind, often experience cross-pressures that can cause a great deal of conflict. This can cause high levels of stress as the young person struggles to resolve the issue, one way or the other.

However, in general parent–peer conflicts are kept to a minimum, as each group exerts their influence in a different domain of the young person's life. This has been shown in a study by Hans Sebald (1986) who conducted a number of interviews with young people, asking them who they would go to for advice on various different issues. He found that whether the adolescent turned to their parents or peers depended a great deal on the type of problem they were faced with. For example, peers were much more influential than parents on issues of clothing, clubbing, social events and most recreational activities. Parents, on the other hand, were more likely to be approached if the young person needed advice on education, career choices, or other future-oriented decisions. These findings relate to research by Youniss and Smollar (1985), which concluded that adolescents and their parents tend to have similar values and attitudes towards important issues. Family conflicts that do arise are normally confined to minor issues, such as untidy rooms, loud music, and household chores.

Write a short essay (one page) describing the positive and negative impact of peers and parents on the social development of adolescents.

Progress exercise

## Cultural differences in adolescent behaviour

As noted earlier, adolescence was traditionally seen as a time of conflict and stress. However, many studies carried out in Western cultures have found that this is not the case. For example, Youniss and Smollar (1985) found that adolescent conflict with parents is often restricted to minor upsets concerning tidiness, loud music and household chores. But are these findings relevant to all cultures? A study by Offer, Ostrov, Howard and Atkinson (1988) surveyed adolescents in a variety of countries including Australia, Bangladesh, Hungary, Israel, Italy, Taiwan, Turkey, USA and West Germany, and found that 91 per cent held no grudges against their parents and a similar number felt their parents were not ashamed of them. These young people appear to be fairly happy with their home lives and do not seem to be experiencing adolescence as a time of great stress. It seems in this instance, that the experience of adolescence is similar across cultures.

### The effect of peers cross-culturally

A possible effect of peers from research carried out in Western cultures is that they provide the adolescent with the security and self-confidence they need to take their final steps towards independence (Steinberg and Silverberg 1986). However in many cultures, particularly Asian cultures such as Chinese, Japanese and Indian, as well as some African cultures, the independence of the individual is seen as unimportant compared to the importance of the family group. Independence and autonomy is not something that young people within these more **collectivist cultures** strive towards (Cole 1992). Likewise in Hispanic cultures young people are more family oriented and less likely to be influenced by peers (DeRosier and Kupersmidt 1991). Similarly, studies conducted in Mexico and Central America found that parents deliberately discourage peer interaction in order to maintain the adolescent's focus on the family (Holtzman et al. 1975). In contrast, the approach of the more **individualistic** Western cultures is to emphasise the importance of the individual over the family group (Guisinger and Blatt 1994), and so encourage the move towards independence during adolescence. Therefore the experiences of young people interacting with their peers in Western cultures appear to be very different from those growing up in other cultures.

### Cultural differences in attitudes towards education

The educational attainment of adolescents from different cultures also shows wide differences. A study by Stevenson and Lee (1990) found that students in Taiwan, China and Japan outperform Western students in maths and reading ability, as well as in other subjects. These findings have been replicated by several studies (McKnight et al. 1987; Stevenson et al. 1993). Although individual differences between students may account for some of these findings, it seems that cultural differences in attitudes towards education are at the heart of it. Within Asian cultures more time is given over to education. Asian students spend more hours per day and more days per year at school, as well as being assigned and completing more homework (Stevenson et al. 1986). Also, both parents and students share a strong belief that hard work at school will bring long-term benefits. Interestingly, research by Crystal et al. (1994) found that, although Asian adolescents are under more pressure to achieve at school than Western adolescents, they exhibit less anxiety and stress about school.

Answer the following questions, quoting the appropriate research:

1   Do the relationships between adolescents and their parents differ cross-culturally?

2   What is the difference between collectivist and individualist societies?

3   Explain why there are cross-cultural differences in school achievement.

Progress exercise

In the final part of this chapter we will focus on the topic of adolescent pregnancy; we will discuss cultural variations in the incidence of adolescent pregnancy; and we will discuss various issues that arise during this time.

## Cultural differences in the occurrence of adolescent pregnancy

In 1988, approximately 13 per cent of adolescent females living in the USA aged between 15 and 19 years became pregnant. From these, 36 per cent ended in abortion, 14 per cent were miscarried, 17 per cent ended in adoption, and 33 per cent stayed with their natural parent/s (Voydanoff and Donnelly 1991). Sadly, unplanned and often unwanted adolescent pregnancies persist, and even though the number of individual cases has been steadily declining over the last decade, the incidence is still very high. In the UK 9.5 per 1000 pregnancies occurred in young women under 16 (DOH 1992). In the USA the incidence was even higher, with the rate being almost double that of other industrialised countries (see Figure 11.2). Why should this be the case? Young Americans are not more sexually active than their peers in other countries, nor are they less likely to have an abortion. In fact, abortion rates are higher in the USA than anywhere else in the world (Brozan 1985). There are two reasons that are normally put forward to account for why adolescents become pregnant. The first is that they perceive some sort of material gain from the pregnancy, normally housing or financial benefit. Several studies have been conducted (e.g. Phoenix 1991; Moore and Rosenthal 1992), but none have found evidence to support this. The second puts forward 'incompetence' as the main reason for adolescent pregnancy, and evidence for this was reported by Phoenix (1991) who found that 82 per cent of young girls had not planned to get pregnant. This finding appears to indicate that young people lack the information they need to make informed decisions about sex. A review of studies by Phoenix (1991) shows that many researchers attribute the higher rates of pregnancy to a cultural ambivalence about sex. The media – television, rock music etc. – contributes to the idea that sexual experimentation is acceptable, and promiscuity is portrayed alongside attractiveness and popularity. Yet at the same time we appear to be reluctant to give teenagers the information they need in order to make informed decisions about sex. Television is often unwilling to broadcast programmes on sex and contraception, and sex education in schools is still an area of contro-versy (especially concerning sexual identities that are not heterosexual). Adolescents report that their parents are often reluctant to discuss sexuality and contraception with them (Morrison 1985). In contrast, countries like Sweden believe that to demystify sex at an early age is the way forward. Sex education at school begins at 7 years old, and by 10 most children have a good understanding not only of reproduction, but also of the various types of contraception available. This approach appears to have a positive effect, as Sweden has one of the lowest rates of adolescent pregnancy. However, a simple rela-tionship between education and rate of adolescent pregnancy must be

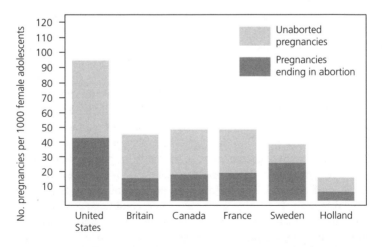

*Figure 11.2* **Adolescent pregnancy rates per 1000 female adolescents**

viewed with caution. The reasons why adolescent pregnancy is higher in some cultures than others is multifactorial. Factors such as academic expectations, higher self-esteem and socio-economic status also play a role. What is apparent is the lack of preventive programmes in countries like the UK and the USA, and this may be something policy makers should take note of and perhaps think of ways of implementing.

Starting and raising a family is highly challenging for most people, but for an adolescent the challenges can be even more severe, and often have long-term negative consequences. Adolescent parents are often still in the process of learning about themselves, receiving an education and thinking about life choices concerning possible career paths, etc. To be faced with parenthood at this time can be a daunting prospect.

### The outcome of adolescent pregnancy

Young women who become pregnant are faced with the most difficult decision they will probably ever have to make: should they raise the child alone, have an abortion, have the child adopted, or move in with their partner and raise a family together. Research has shown that various factors can have an effect on the final decision. These include religious values, racial differences and family background. Voydanoff and Donnelly (1991) found that black adolescent women from female-headed families, whose parents had not graduated from high school, were most likely to choose single parenthood over abortion or a partnership with the infant's father. Generally, black adolescents would be more likely to raise their child. In comparison, research by Marsiglio and Menaghan (1990) found that white adolescent females (especially those with educated parents) were more likely to choose abortion over birth. Young people with firm religious beliefs (regardless of ethnicity) were more likely to choose birth over abortion. Also, an adolescent's perception of the expectations other people have of them (such as parents) can have a large impact on the final decision they make (Brazzell and Acock 1988).

### The effects of adolescent pregnancy on the child

Research has shown that the children of parents aged 17 or under score less on tests of cognitive ability than children of older parents (Dash

1989). Also, there is a tendency for these children to have lower IQ scores. These children have been found to be generally more hostile, and to exhibit greater over-activity and lack of impulse control, than similar age children of older parents (Burton 1990). Other research has found that the chances of these children growing up in disruptive homes, having lower academic aptitude as teenagers, and of repeating the pattern of early parenthood is also very high (Baldwin and Cain 1980). Compared to the offspring of older parents, these children are more likely to suffer from behavioural problems and delinquency when they reach their own adolescence (Furstenberg et al. 1987). The following section looks at the possibilities of alleviating some of the negative outcomes of adolescent pregnancy.

### Can the negative effects be reduced?

Berk (1997) found that only 50 per cent of females who gave birth before they were 18 years old finished high school, compared to 96 per cent who didn't. This lack of education can mean that many young mothers are unable to find work to support themselves and their child, and as a consequence must rely on the support of the state. This can mean living in a state of near poverty, with little or no hope of changing the situation they are in. It is perhaps these findings that give the clearest indication of some effective ways of helping young parents, by encouraging them to provide a positive environment for their children.

One of the reasons many young women don't return to education after having a child is often related to poverty and lack of childcare facilities. It is here that social policy could have a positive effect by offering financial and practical help, and thereby creating more choice for young mothers. Research has shown that if adolescent mothers are able to return to education, and live in an environment with good social support systems, then the outcome for them and their child can be good (Berk 1997).

A final point worth noting is that all of the above discussion refers to adolescents who have unplanned and/or unwanted pregnancies. Young couples who make the choice to start a family early and have the appropriate resources available to them are just as likely to produce happy, well-adjusted children as any other age group.

Design a leaflet that informs young people about adolescent pregnancy. Describe some of the negative effects and add some research findings. Try to make your leaflet interesting and fairly detailed. Give it to some of your friends to read.

## Summary

In this final chapter on adolescence we have discussed the influence of peers and parents on the development of the young person. We have seen how relationships between peers have a strong effect on the development of the young person. We have also seen how relationships are affected by gender: girls are more likely to have one-to-one friend-ships with other girls, while boys are more likely to form into groups. Relationships are often driven by the need for conformity, and their influence can be positive or negative. We have compared these findings with the experiences of adolescents living in other cultures. We have found that in some ways the experiences of young people from different cultures are similar, such as their relationships with their parents, while in others they are very different, such as the influence of peers. We have also looked at adolescent pregnancy and seen how cultures vary in sex education and incidence of adolescent pregnancy. We have discussed the effects of starting a family at a young age, and have concluded that education, the media and parents all have an important role to play. This is mainly by providing information and support systems that open up the possibilities and help young people make the right decisions for themselves, and for the futures they hope to achieve.

## Further reading

Bornstein, M.H. and Lamb, M.E. (eds) *Developmental Psychology: An advanced textbook*, Hillsdale NJ: Lawrence Erlbaum Associates. A detailed but highly readable book that looks at cultural differences in development.

Musick, S.J. (1993) *Young, poor and pregnant: the psychology of teenage motherhood*, New York: Vail-Ballou Press. An absorbing account of the problems facing teenage mothers.

Elster, A.B. and Lamb, M.E. (1986) *Adolescent Fatherhood*, Hillsdale NJ: Lawrence Erlbaum Associates. An interesting book highlighting the effects of becoming a teenage father, both positive and negative.

# 12

# Study aids

## IMPROVING YOUR ESSAY-WRITING SKILLS

At this point in the book you have acquired the knowledge necessary to tackle the exam itself. Answering exam questions is a skill which this chapter shows you how to improve. Examiners obviously have first-hand knowledge about what goes wrong in exams. For example, candidates frequently do not answer the question which has been set, rather, they answer the one that they hoped would come up, or they do not make effective use of the knowledge they have but just 'dump their psychology' on the page and hope the examiner will sort it out for them. A grade C answer usually contains appropriate material but tends to be limited in detail and commentary. To lift such an answer to a grade A or B may require no more than a little more detail, better use of material and coherent organisation. It is important to appreciate it may not involve writing at any greater length, but might even necessitate the elimination of passages which do not add to the quality of the answer and some elaboration of those which do.

By studying the essays presented in this chapter and the examiner's comments, you can learn how to turn your grade C answer into a grade A. Typically it only involves an extra 4 marks out of 24. Please note that marks given by the examiner in the practice essays should be used as a guide only and are not definitive. They represent the 'raw' marks which would be likely to be given to answers to AQA (A) questions.

In the AQA (A) examination, an examiner would award a maximum of 12 marks for knowledge and understanding (called Assessment Objective 1/AO1) and 12 marks for evaluation, analysis and commentary (Assessment Objective 2/AO2). The details of this marking scheme are given in Appendix C of Paul Humphreys' title in this series, *Exam Success in AEB Psychology,* and the forthcoming title *Exam Success in AQA(A) Psychology*. Remember that these are the raw marks and not the same as those given on the examination certificate received ultimately by the candidate. This is because all examining boards are required to use a common standardised system called the Uniform Mark Scale (UMS) which adjusts all raw scores to a single standard across all boards.

The essays given here are notionally written by an 18 year old in thirty minutes and marked bearing that in mind. It is important when writing to such a tight time limit that you make every sentence count. Each essay in this chapter is followed by detailed comments about its strengths and weaknesses. The most common problems to watch out for are:

- Failure to answer the question but reproducing a model answer to a similar question which you have pre-learned.
- Not delivering the right balance between description and evaluation/analysis. Remember they are always weighted 50/50.
- Writing 'everything you know' about a topic in the hope that something will get credit and the examiner will sort your work out for you. Remember that excellence demands selectivity, so improvements can often be made by removing material which is irrelevant to the question set and elaborating material which is relevant.
- Failing to use your material effectively. It is not enough to place the information on the page but you must also show the examiner that you are using it to make a particular point.

For more ideas on how to write good essays you should consult *Exam Success in AEB Psychology* and the forthcoming title *Exam Success in AQA(A) Psychology* (both by Paul Humphreys) in this series.

## Practice essay 1

## Discuss one explanation of personality development. (24 marks)

*Examiner's advice*

*In this question you are required to both describe and then evaluate one explanation of personality development. If you know more than one explanation you can use this material by describing one and then using the other explanation as a form of evaluation or contrast. Other ways of evaluating an explanation are by looking at research evidence that may be supportive or non-supportive. You might also consider applications of the explanation, for example to personality tests.*

*Candidate's answer*

Personality is a difficult concept to explain as it could refer to any number of aspects of a person. For example, some psychologists see personality as a fixed part of a person's makeup, such as Eysenck's personality theory. Whereas others see it as changing and flexible, and tied to a person's experiences in life.

In this essay I will focus on only one approach to the study of personality, that of Eysenck. Eysenck began his research into personality by observing the behaviours of psychiatric patients that he was working with. He noticed that many of their behaviours seemed to follow a particular pattern according to the type of mental illness they were suffering from. He applied these behaviours to a statistical procedure known as factor analysis and managed to isolate clusters of behaviours or what he called factors of behaviours that together formed a dimension. An example of some of these factors were things like talkativeness, liveliness, or shyness, anxiety, etc. These factors formed the dimension of introversion/extraversion, so that a person who was very outgoing and talkative would be deemed an extravert, while a shy and retiring person would be deemed an introvert. Eysenck eventually isolated two different dimensions to account for human personality. These were extraversion/introversion (E) and neuroticism/stability (N). Eysenck also devised a questionnaire that could be used to categorise a person according to where they scored on the dimensions. A person would gain a score on both dimensions in different places. For example a person might be a neurotic introvert, or a neurotic extravert, or they might be a stable introvert or a stable extravert. Eysenck also isolated a third dimension known as psychoticism, but this one has not been as researched as the other two and is more controversial due to its apparent link with mental illness.

Eysenck found that both (E) and (N) were normally distributed among the population. One criticism of Eysenck is that he believed personality was a genetic part of a person's makeup and so was biological. He believed that introverts become easily excited during their day-to-day lives because they have a very sensitive nervous system, and so to avoid over-stimulation seek out quiet and calm places, and vice versa with extraverts. However if this were the case then it could be expected that introverts could be easily taught specific behaviours (conditioned) using a stimulus response approach as they are so sensitive, and react so quickly to a stimulus, whereas extraverts should prove to be very difficult to condition. Lots of research has looked at this (e.g. Gale 1981) and found that this is not the case, only half of the sample used were able to be conditioned according to their personality type. Also if there were a biological basis to personality, you would expect identical twins to score on the same dimension, again this was only found to be the case in 50 per cent (Loehlin et al. 1988). Another way of evaluating Eysenck's research is to look at the validity of the questionnaire he devised known as Eysenck's personality inventory. If the questionnaire is measuring what it says it measures then its validity will be high. Furnham (1981) found that the questionnaire was a good predictor of behaviour, for example those people assessed as extraverts did prefer stimulating social activities such as competitions, whereas those assessed as neurotics tended to avoid these sorts of situations. Also Gibson found that the questionnaire was able to rate individuals in a similar way to how they rated themselves and to how their friends rated them. Both of these studies show that Eysenck's questionnaire is valid.

However other researchers such as Heim (1970) have argued that using a questionnaire is very restrictive as the person can only answer yes or no to the questions and may want to answer maybe or sometimes. This means that the answers they give may not be what they would actually mean.

Overall, it seems that Eysenck's ideas about personality being part of our biology do not stand up to research and are not properly explained, but his method of measuring personality (his questionnaire) is a good method and does have validity.

### Examiner's comment

*The first half of the essay fails to appropriately address the question. The candidate is required to provide an explanation of personality development whereas this is more of a description of how Eysenck conducted the research which led to the formulation of the theory. The material is not* irrelevant *but it doesn't really explain how personality develops.*

*The first criticism (about biological causation) starts with credit-worthy material describing the theory and then offers commentary in the form of attempts to verify the biological hypothesis. This commentary is informed and well elaborated.*

*The second criticism is again of the methodology and not the explanation itself. Thus, this again is only partially relevant. However, some credit would be given for this as it is an appropriate evaluative point.*

*The conclusion does not offer much more than has already been said.*

*In general Skill AO1 is limited and not always focused on the question. It might receive a mark of 5. The Skill AO2 is very limited in scope. What is relevant is excellent but there is not enough for more than 6 marks. The total of 11 marks would be equivalent to a grade D.*

### Practice essay 2

## Discuss psychological research into the development of gender roles. (24 marks)

### Examiner's advice

*The injunction 'discuss' requires you to describe research into the development of gender roles. 'Research' may be either theories or studies. 'Discuss' also entails evaluation of the research. If you have*

**151**

*described research studies then you may evaluate their methodology. If you have described theories, then you may use research studies as a form of evaluation.*

### Candidate's answer

An individual's gender identity is tied to their sense of being male or female and of belonging to that particular group in society. The way a person reaches this sense of identity comes from a process of socialisation that takes account of the separate roles carried out by males and females. These separate roles are referred to as gender roles, and are specific to the culture in which they are learned.

Bandura has shown how children model the behaviour of those around them but are particularly drawn to the behaviours of same-sex models. For example, boys learn from their fathers that attending football matches or race circuits are male behaviours while girls learn from observing their mothers that shopping and cooking are typical female behaviours. However these gender stereotypes are not as rigid as they were in the past, and in fact gender roles are changing rapidly. These days it is perfectly acceptable for females to both attend and play games like football, and many males stay at home and care for the house and children. So Bandura's social learning theory can be used to explain how we learn the gender roles that eventually form our gender identity.

An experiment carried out by Perry and Bussey (1979) has shown that it isn't so much the frequency that a behaviour is observed that predicts whether that behaviour is learned or not, but whether it is viewed as gender appropriate. For example, they took a sample of children and exposed them to four female and four male models choosing an item from a selection of two (an apple and a banana). Afterwards the children were asked which item they themselves would prefer. It was found that if all four of the female models and all four of the male models chose the same item, then the children of the same sex would also choose that item as the one they preferred. If, however, only two of the female models and two of the male models chose the same item then the children chose indiscriminately. This shows children will only imitate a same-sex behaviour if it is one they see as normally performed by that gender. For example, seeing a male wearing a dress is not a common sight and so may not be imitated by same-sex observers. If however, all men start to wear dresses then it becomes a frequently-viewed behaviour, and will be more likely to be copied by same-sex observers (i.e. the children), and become a gender-appropriate behaviour or gender role.

Fagot (1978) observed children aged between 20 and 24 months in a home environment and found that girls were reinforced for different behaviours than boys, even at that young age. She found that girls were encouraged to dance, stay near parents and ask for help, and discouraged from rough-and-tumble play. Boys, on the other hand, were encouraged to play roughly, discouraged from asking for help, dancing, or playing with stereotypical female toys such as baby dolls. This shows that boys and girls are socialised differently from a very young age and learn what is appropriate behaviour very early on in their lives. Also the way girls and boys are dressed differently reinforces the differences between the genders and makes sure that strangers will respond to them in ways that are considered appropriate for each sex. For example, a young girl in a pink dress may be told she is pretty, while a boy in a suit handsome, this again reinforces gender role expectations.

Cross-cultural studies also highlight the effect of learning and culture on gender roles. Mead (1935) observed the behaviour of three different ethnic groups: the Arapesh, the Mundugumor and the Tchambuli people. She found that within each group the gender roles of males and females were very different. For example, in the Arapesh culture the roles were very equal and quite similar, whereas in the Tchambuli culture the females were very aggressive and competitive whereas the male gender roles were to nurture the children and take care of the household (a reversal of Western gender roles).

Overall, it seems we learn our gender roles rather than them being innate and genetically prescribed. As noted earlier the changing face of society means that what was a typical female gender role twenty years ago is no longer seen that way. Nowadays it is quite normal for the male to take care of the house and children, and the female to be the main breadwinner. Gender roles are becoming more and more unisex, which of course is also down to learning.

### Examiner's comment

*The candidate has presented a number of research studies in reason-able detail, as required. There is also some attempt to talk more generally about explanations (theories) of gender role development. It might have been useful throughout to maintain a focus on gender roles rather than talking about gender more generally. For example, at the start of the second paragraph there is a description of how boys model their behaviour on their fathers. This could have been 'gender roles' rather than 'gender behaviours' in order for the essay to read as specifically appropriate to this question rather than a prepared answer.*

*The commentary/evaluation is rather weaker. Both the second and third paragraphs finish with a consideration of what the research demonstrates but there is no attempt to look at the value of the research in terms, for example, of the methodology used. Evaluation might also be achieved through a consideration of alternative explanations for gender role development, e.g. the biological view.*

*The Skill AO1 content is fairly well detailed but slightly limited, for 8 marks. The Skill AO2 is reasonable but limited, for 5 marks. The total of 13 marks is equivalent to a Grade C.*

## Practice essay 3

### (a) Describe research into social development in adolescence. (12 marks) (b) Assess the extent to which such development is related to cultural differences. (12 marks)

#### Examiner's advice

*In part (a) a straightforward description of research (studies or theories) is required that explains social development in adolescence. The concept of 'social development' is broad and virtually any theory could be made relevant. There is a danger of trying to cover too much material in this part of the question and thus sacrificing depth for breadth (depth–breadth trade-off) and this would prevent achieving top marks. You need to achieve a good amount of detail rather than trying to write a bit about everything you know.*

*In part (b) you are required to consider whether there is an association between social development in adolescence and cultural differences. Since this is a Skill AO2 question you must ensure that you do not simply describe such differences but assess the extent to which there are (or are not) cultural differences – thus assessing the extent to which development is related to cultural practices.*

*Candidate's answer*

a) Adolescence means to 'grow into maturity' and during this period of growth many changes take place that are not only physical, but also psychological. Traditionally, according to Hall (1904) adolescence was thought to be a time of 'storm and stress', whereby the individual suffers extreme mood swings and unpredictable behaviour. However more recent research has shown this not to be the case. A theory by Coleman (1974) known as 'focal theory' explains that although young people tend to go through lots of changes in their lives, they have the ability to focus on them one at a time. This means that they are able to deal with each new change as it occurs, rather than trying to grapple with a multitude of changes at once, and so presumably do not experience a time of storm and stress. Research has provided evidence for this in the form of a study of 800 boys and girls aged 11 to 17 years. Coleman and Hendry (1990) conducted interviews on this sample and asked them to talk about subjects they found stressful, such as self-image, career choices, peer, sexual and parental relationships. They found that each area of discussion had a different level of importance, reaching a high level or peak of importance at different ages. For example, worries about peer relationships were more important at an earlier age than occupational choice. This backs up Coleman's focal theory by showing that individuals do indeed focus on different things at different times during the adolescent period.

Another area of social development that has been researched is that of self-perception. During adolescence young people start to become more aware of themselves. Worries about appearance, height and weight begin. A study that has looked at this was conducted by Brooks Gunn and Warren (1988). They found that females are more likely to worry about appearance and like to be thought of as attractive. Any physical changes they experienced were okay as long as they were in line with the 'feminine ideal' that is constantly being portrayed through the media. An example of this 'feminine ideal' is having breasts, but not being fat. Therefore an adolescent who suddenly begins to develop breasts would not worry, whereas one who begins to put on weight would.

A final area of social development concerns the increased incidence of teenage pregnancy. In 1988 13 per cent of females between the ages of 15 and 19 became pregnant. Why this should be the case has been the question researchers have attempted to answer. Morrison (1985) believes the answer lies in society's reluctance to allow adolescents the information they need to make informed decisions about their sexuality, including how they want to express it. The media constantly show sexual experimentation as a cool thing to do, but hardly ever broadcast programmes about sex or contraception. Added to this is the finding by Berk (1997) that of those adolescents who become teenage mothers and fathers only 50 per cent finish their education. This has wide implications for their futures as they will be less likely to find a decent job and support their young family in a decent way.

b) Culturally there are differences in the social development of adolescents. One factor is the different approaches to life that various cultures have. For example, Western culture is focused on individual development and achievement. This is reflected in Coleman's focal theory that sees the outcome of any social changes experienced by the adolescent as dependent on how they themselves are able to resolve or come to terms with the change. However, in other cultures the resolution of social change is often down to the family unit or even the local community, rather than the individual adolescent. Eastern cultures are far more collective, and the adolescent is not given the same freedom to make their own choices. In collective cultures the benefit of the family is put before the benefit of any one individual, and each family member plays their part in this. This approach to life makes for a far less selfish and possibly less stressed society.

Another difference in social development concerns the area of teenage pregnancy. Other cultures are far more open and informative than British culture. For example, in Sweden sex education begins at 7 years old and so by the time the individual reaches adolescence they are well informed as to the consequences of their actions. This means that fewer young people become pregnant due to ignorance, in fact Sweden has the lowest rate of teenage pregnancy in the world.

A final area of social development in teenagers that shows cultural differences is that of appearance. As stated earlier teenagers often become worried about their appearance if it goes against the 'ideal' portrayed through the media. In other cultures this ideal can be very different, for example in some African cultures being fat is seen as being beautiful, and some families go to extreme lengths to achieve this, such as sending their daughters to fattening houses. However, this shows that whatever the cultural norm, the aspect of trying to imitate it is similar across some cultures.

Overall, there do appear to be cultural differences in social development of adolescents but also some similarities.

*Examiner's comment*

*The candidate has started well in defining the area by explaining some traditional beliefs about social development in adolescence. A number of research studies have then been presented in reasonable detail. However, the candidate has to some degree sacrificed depth for breadth and for this reason will not achieve the top mark in this section. It would have been better to give fewer studies/theories of social development during adolescence, and concentrated more on the detail.*

*The commentary/evaluation is again rather weak, although some interesting points are raised. For example, the candidate discusses how cross-culturally not all adolescents have the same freedom or autonomy to make their own choices. This would have been an excellent point had it been backed up with research evidence.*

*The Skill AO1 content is reasonably detailed and accurate, reasonably constructed but limited, for 7/8 marks. The Skill AO2 is reasonable but limited, with material used effectively and with more than some evidence of coherent collaboration, for 7 marks. The total of 15 marks is equivalent to a Grade B.*

## KEY RESEARCH SUMMARIES

*Article 1*

**Bandura A., Ross D., & Ross S.A. (1961). *Transmission of aggression through imitation of aggressive models. Journal of Abnormal and Social Psychology*, 63, 575–82.**

*Aim*

The overall aim of this study is to demonstrate that learning can occur through the imitation of observed behaviours, and further that this learned behaviour be exhibited in the absence of the original model.

The specific aims of this particular study are as follows:

1 Children who observe aggressive models will show significantly more imitative aggressive behaviour than those who observe non-aggressive models, or no models at all.

2 Children who observe non-aggressive models will show significantly less aggressive behaviour than those who observe aggressive models or no models at all.

3 Children are more likely to imitate the behaviour of a same-sex model than a model of the opposite sex.

4 Boys are more likely to behave aggressively than girls are after observing an aggressive model, especially when that model is male.

## Participants

72 children took part in the study, consisting of 36 girls and 36 boys aged between 37 and 69 months. The mean age was 52 months. The models were one adult male and one adult female.

## Design

This was a laboratory experiment, in which the independent variable (IV) was the type of model observed. There were three main conditions – aggressive condition, non-aggressive condition and control:

Aggressive condition – the children who took part in this condition were exposed to an aggressive model either of the same sex or of the opposite sex.

Non-aggressive condition – here the children were exposed to a non-aggressive model again either of the same or the opposite sex.

Control condition – these children were not exposed to any model.

## Procedure

In the two experimental conditions, children were individually shown into a room containing a number of toys. One corner of the room was set out as a child's play area with a table and chair, some potato prints and picture stickers. The child was led to this corner. The adult model was led to another corner of the room also containing a table and chair, plus a mallet, tinker toys and a five foot inflatable bobo doll. The experimenter then left the room.

In the non-aggressive condition the adult (either male or female) played with the tinker toys in a quiet subdued manner and ignored the bobo doll.

In the aggressive condition the adult (either male or female) started to play with the tinker toys but after one minute turned to the bobo doll and behaved aggressively towards it in a stylised way. This consisted of a) sitting on bobo and repeatedly punching it on the nose, b) striking bobo on the head with a mallet, c) throwing bobo in the air and kicking it around the room. The model was also verbally aggressive towards the bobo, saying things like, 'sock him in the nose', 'throw him in the air' and 'pow', and verbally non-aggressive with 'he keeps coming back for more' and 'he sure is a tough fella'.

All children (including the control) were then led individually to a second room and subjected to mild aggressive arousal. This consisted of being shown a number of highly attractive toys, and then being told that these toys were reserved for good children and they themselves would not be able to play with them.

All children were then led to the final room which contained both aggressive toys (a bobo doll, a mallet, dartguns) and non-aggressive toys (a tea set, dolls, colouring paper). Each child was observed for twenty minutes through a one-way mirror.

Observations were made at five-second intervals allowing 240 response units for each child. The following behaviours were recorded:

Three measures of imitative aggression:

1  Imitative physical aggression
2  Imitative verbal aggression
3  Imitative non-aggressive responses

Two measures of partial imitative aggression:

1  Mallet aggression
2  Sits on bobo

Three measures of non-imitative aggression:

1  Punches bobo
2  Other physical or verbal aggression
3  Aggressive gun play

*Findings*

See Table 12.1 for mean responses. The four main results were as follows:

1 Children in the aggressive model condition showed significantly more imitative aggression than those in the non-aggressive condition.
2 Overall boys showed more aggressive acts than girls did.
3 Boys in the aggressive condition showed more aggressive acts if the model was male.
4 Girls in the aggressive condition showed more physical aggression if the model was male and more verbal aggression if the model was female.

*Conclusions*

Bandura and his colleagues have shown in this study that behaviours can be learned via observation of a social model. They have also demonstrated that the learned behaviour can be exhibited even when the model is no longer present. Lastly, it does appear that boys are generally more aggressive than girls, but whether this is an innate feature of male behaviour or learned is still in question.

*Discussion*

One of the issues to arise from this study is the effect that the gender of the model had on the children. Bandura, Ross, and Ross noted that the aggression of the female model had a confusing effect. For example, one of the children said, 'You should have seen what that girl did in there. She was acting just like a man . . .', while another child said, 'Who is that lady? That's not the way for a lady to behave . . .'. However, the aggression of the male model was seen as perfectly acceptable, and led to comments such as, 'That man is a strong fighter . . .' and 'He's a good fighter like Daddy'. It seems that behaviours considered appropriate for each gender are strongly related to cultural stereotypes even at this early age.

In terms of the nature/nurture debate, the study shows that aggressive behaviour can be learned. However, it does not offer conclusive evidence that any features of aggression (particularly those exhibited by the male participant) are innately acquired. As shown above from the comments made by the children, the expectation that males will behave more aggressively than females is already formed.

However, we should remember that the situation these children

**Table 12.1** Mean aggression scores for experimental and control subjects

| Response category | Experimental groups | | | | Control Groups |
| --- | --- | --- | --- | --- | --- |
| | Aggressive | | Non-aggressive | | |
| | Female model | Male model | Female model | Male model | |
| **Imitative physical aggression** | | | | | |
| Female subjects | 5.5 | 7.2 | 2.5 | 0.0 | 1.2 |
| Male subjects | 12.4 | 25.8 | 0.2 | 1.5 | 2.0 |
| **Imitative verbal aggression** | | | | | |
| Female subjects | 13.7 | 2.0 | 0.3 | 0.0 | 0.7 |
| Male subjects | 4.3 | 12.7 | 1.1 | 0.0 | 1.7 |
| **Mallet aggression** | | | | | |
| Female subjects | 17.2 | 18.7 | 0.5 | 0.5 | 13.1 |
| Male subjects | 15.5 | 28.8 | 18.7 | 6.7 | 13.5 |
| **Punches Bobo** | | | | | |
| Female subjects | 6.3 | 16.5 | 5.8 | 4.3 | 11.7 |
| Male subjects | 18.9 | 11.9 | 15.6 | 14.8 | 15.7 |
| **Non-imitative aggression** | | | | | |
| Female subjects | 21.3 | 8.4 | 7.2 | 1.4 | 6.1 |
| Male subjects | 16.2 | 36.7 | 26.1 | 22.3 | 24.6 |
| **Aggressive gun play** | | | | | |
| Female subjects | 1.8 | 4.5 | 2.6 | 2.5 | 3.7 |
| Male subjects | 7.3 | 15.9 | 8.9 | 16.7 | 14.3 |

Source: Bandura, Ross & Ross (1961)

found themselves in is not a normal one (observing a stranger beat up a plastic doll), and the long-term effects of the learned behaviour are unknown.

DISCUSSION QUESTIONS

1 How was the aggressive behaviour of the children measured?
2 How else could the aggressive behaviour be measured?
3 How was aggression expressed in the study?
4 What are the implications of constructing a study where the aggression is more realistic?

## Article 2

**Bem S, L. (1974). The measurement of psychological androgyny.**
***Journal of Consulting and Clinical Psychology*, 42, 155–62.**

*Aim*

Bem challenges the traditional idea of femininity–masculinity, whereby a person can be described as *either* feminine *or* masculine, but not both. She argues for the existence of a third gender identity whereby a person can be *both* masculine and feminine, which she describes as psychological androgyny. The aim of this study is to develop a questionnaire that can account for and measure all three types of sex-role behaviour – masculine, feminine and androgynous. This questionnaire is known as the Bem Sex Role Inventory or BSRI.

*Participants*

Different participants were used at different stages of the development of the questionnaire.

During the item selection stage, 100 Stanford University students were used (50 male and 50 female) to evaluate the items.

At the stage of administering the questionnaire, 723 Stanford students (279 females and 444 males) and 194 junior college students (77 female and 117 male) took part.

At the retest stage, 56 Stanford students (28 female and 28 male) took part.

This article documents the development of a psychological question-naire. The process involved two stages of development, consisting of item selection and psychometric analysis. These are described in the procedure below.

To start with, Bem and a group of students chose 200 words depicting personality characteristics, e.g. competitive, yielding etc. All of the words were thought to be positive descriptions of either feminine or masculine traits. Following this, 100 students rated the words on seven-point Likert scale (1 = not at all desirable, 7 = extremely desirable) for males and females in an American culture. 50 students (25 male/25 female) rated the words for males, while the other 50 students (25 male/25 female) rated the words for females.

If a word was rated as desirable for females by both male and female judges, then it was included as a possible 'feminine' item. The same procedure was used for the masculine items, and eventually 20 items for each gender were selected for the final questionnaire. Twenty neutral items (neither masculine nor feminine) were added to provide a measure of social desirability in self-rating. This resulted in a questionnaire of sixty items, known as the Bem Sex Role Inventory (BSRI).

When filling in the BSRI, participants are asked to rate themselves on each of the sixty items using a seven-point Likert scale (1 = never or almost never true, 7 = always or almost always true). A participant's Masculine ('M') score is obtained by adding up their ratings for the 20 masculine items, while their feminine ('F') score is obtained by adding up their ratings for the 20 feminine items. Participants also receive an Androgyny ('A') score which is obtained by subtracting the masculine ('M') score from the feminine ('F') score, the closer the final 'A' score is to zero the more androgynous the person is. A high positive score on 'A' indicates a feminine sex-typed person, while a high negative score on 'A' indicates a masculine sex-typed person.

Bem also provides a more complicated way of calculating the 'A' score but accepts that a simpler method (as described above) can be used instead.

## Psychometric Analysis

Bem analysed the reliability and validity of her questionnaire in various ways, three of which will be discussed in this summary. She tested the internal reliability of the scale by checking that individual's scores were consistent throughout the scale. For example, if a person scored high on a feminine item, then if the scale is reliable, it is probable that they would score high on other feminine items. Bem's analysis confirmed that the questionnaire was consistent in this way, therefore was internally reliable.

She also tested the external reliability of the scale. To do this she re-administered the test to 56 of the original 723 Stanford University students, four weeks after they had completed it the first time round. This is known as **test-retest reliability**. If the questionnaire had external reliability, the scores of the participants should be more or less the same. In order to compare the re-test scores with the original scores Bem calculated a correlation coefficient. This would show how closely the two scores of each participant matched. A perfect correlation would yield a coefficient of 1, whereas no correlation would yield a correlation of 0. She found that all scores had a correlation coefficient of at least 0.90 allowing her to claim a high level of test-retest reliability.

Finally, Bem looked at the **construct validity** of her questionnaire. This would show whether the questionnaire matches the theory behind it. Bem had originally asserted that the dimensions of masculinity and femininity exist as completely separate entities. Therefore they could only be assessed using an orthogonal scale rather than a traditional continuum (see Chapter 8 for a discussion of this). If this was a valid assertion then participant's 'M' and 'F' scores should bear no relation to each other. After calculating a correlation coefficient for the 'F' and 'M' scores of the Stanford students Bem found values of close to 0. This supports her original assertions of independent dimensions and means that her scale has high construct validity as it supports the theory behind it.

Bem was able to develop a questionnaire that could measure masculinity, femininity and androgyny as separate entities that may co-exist within an individual. Using psychometric analysis Bem was able to illustrate both internal and external reliability.

In terms of validity this summary has only considered construct validity, whereby the theory behind the questionnaire is to some extent proven. However, other types of validity such as **concurrent validity** were shown to be very weak in terms of the BRSI and other measures. Bem simply concluded that this was because the other scales were measuring something different, e.g. masculinity and femininity were constructed on a continuum, rather than as separate entities.

How else could the validity of the scale be tested? Some have suggested that the way a scale is developed should be examined to gain some insight into its validity. Bem certainly took a great deal of care and attention while developing her scale, involving a large number of people in the process. However, it is worth noting that all those involved were of a Western culture, and so the scale may not be applicable to other cultures. Bem herself does admit that the scale is culturally specific. In addition, the sample itself although large was rather narrow, as all participants were students. Lastly, the time that the construction of the scale took place (1970s) would have had an impact on the type of personality characteristic that participants selected as positive or negative for males and/or females.

Overall, we can say that Bem's BSRI is a reliable measure of sex role behaviour, but its validity is historically and culturally tied.

DISCUSSION QUESTIONS

1  What is meant by the terms validity and reliability?
2  Why should we be cautious of the validity of Bem's scale in terms of its historical and cultural context?
3  How did Bem test the reliability of her scale?
4  How might Bem make her scale more valid cross-culturally?

# Glossary

*The first occurrence of each of these terms is highlighted in **bold** type in the main text.*

**anorexia nervosa** An eating disorder characterised by obsessive concern with one's weight.

**anti-social behaviour** Social behaviours that are non-cooperative in nature.

**autonomic nervous system (ANS)** Part of the nervous system concerned with stress reactions.

**autonomy** A sense of independence and the freedom to make choices.

**behaviourism** A school of psychology founded by J.B. Watson where the focus of study is on observable behaviour to the exclusion of any internal mental processes.

**bulimia nervosa** An eating disorder characterised by repeated episodes of 'binge' eating followed by vomiting.

**castration fear** During the resolution of the Oedipal complex the child has a fear of castration.

**clinical depression** A person who has been clinically diagnosed as suffering from depression.

**cliques** Small groups of close friends of mixed gender.

**cognitivism** A psychological approach that is concerned with mental processes such as memory, perception, problem solving and language.

**collectivist cultures** A culture that emphasises the group (as in the community) rather than the individual.

**compensation** Used by Bandura to mean making up for perceived failure by a pretence of superiority.

**concurrent validity** To test the reliability of a test by correlating it with an existing test that claims to measure the same thing.

**conditionability** The ease with which a person can be conditioned/ taught to behave in a specific way.

**conformity** Term meaning a tendency to 'go along with the group', to attempt to act in ways consistent with the majority.

**conscience** According to Freud's theory this is part of the superego which is concerned with what is wrong or bad.

**conscious** Being aware of internal and external events.

**conservation** A Piagetian term used to describe the ability to understand that although the shape of something may change its quantity may not.

**construct validity** To check for a relationship between the theory underlying the test and the test itself. For example, Eysenck's theory states that extroverts have less arousal than introverts. If this were shown to be true it would provide some construct validity for his test.

**continuum** Any variable capable of being represented as a continuous series.

**control group** A separate group used in an investigation against which to compare experimental groups.

**crisis** A term used in Erikson's whole life theory to describe the specific problem facing individuals as they negotiate each stage of development.

**cross-pressures** Conflicting pressures on the way an individual should behave. This may be experienced during adolescence when the expectations of parents and peers may conflict.

**defence mechanisms** Unconscious strategies used by people, often involving the distortion of reality, to protect themselves from guilt or anxiety.

**delusions of grandeur** The misguided belief that we are far greater than any other mere human.

**demand characteristics** Features of the experimental setting that may cause the subject to behave in particular ways.

**determinism** A belief that all human behaviour is caused by forces, whether internal or external, over which one has no control.

**deviant peer group** One who endorses anti-social behaviours, such as criminal activities.

**drives** According to Freud, behaviours that are driven by unconscious, instinctual needs and desires.

**ecological validity** How meaningful (in the real world) findings from research are.

**ego** According to Freud this is the part of the personality that works on the reality principle, and aims to strike a balance between the demands of the id and the superego.

**ego defence mechanisms** If trying to maintain a balance between the id and superego becomes too difficult, the ego protects itself from too much anxiety by blocking or distorting the flood of impulses from the id and superego and turning them into something more acceptable.

**ego ideal** Part of the ego concerned with what is right and good.

**empirical evidence** Evidence based on replicable research.

**epigenetic principle** A term used to indicate that development follows a predetermined order of stages.

**escapism** A term used to describe an escape from reality.

**ethnocentrism** The tendency to view one's own ethnic group and its social norms as the basis for evaluative judgements concerning the practices of other ethnic groups.

**factor analysis** A statistical method used to isolate common factors of behaviour.

**fanaticism** This is when a person becomes so involved in a particular role in society, that they lose tolerance for anything else.

**fixated** According to Freud, if a child fails to negotiate a stage of psychosexual development they can become stuck at that stage. For example, an adult fixated at the oral stage may enjoy smoking, or sucking lollipops.

**free association** A therapeutic method used by psychoanalysts whereby the client is encouraged to talk about whatever comes to mind. This may or may not follow a prompt from the therapist.

**gender identity** A person's sense of being male or female and of belonging to that particular group in society.

**gender roles** The separate roles expected of males and females.

**gender nonschematic** A person who does not order their world according to gender categories. For example, a gender nonschematic person would not consider gender as playing any part in determining the roles performed by males and females.

**gender schema** A child's set of ideas or stereotypes about each gender that develops and changes as the child grows and learns.

**gender schematic** A person who orders their world according to gender categories. For example a gender schematic person would assume that males and females have separate roles in society.

**generalisability** The degree that a finding or theory can be applied to an entire class or category of events, objects or phenomena.

**hope** According to Erikson, the virtue of hope means to believe that even when things are going wrong they will turn out alright in the end.

**humanists** A school of thought concerned with an individual's own subjective perceptions and feelings about their own experiences.

**hypothetical construct** An explanation based on a theory or idea that has not been proven.

**id** According to Freud, this is the part of the personality that is biologically determined and works on the pleasure principle.

**identity crisis** According to Erikson's theory, an identity crisis describes the role confusion felt by most young people during adolescence.

**idiographic** An approach which concentrates on the detailed study of an individual or individuals.

**inactivity** A state of apathy and a withdrawal from participation.

**individualistic** This is where the emphasis is on the individual rather than society as a whole.

**ingroup/outgroup** In terms of gender this would mean the ingroup you belong to (your gender group) and the outgroup you don't belong to (the opposite gender group). This can be applied to any other groups in society such as ethnic groups, work groups, social groups, age groups, etc. For example, in terms of Tottenham football team supporters the ingroup would be Tottenham supporters while the outgroup would be the other team supporters.

**instincts** Behaviours which are genetic and not controlled by conscious decision-making processes.

**introversion/extroversion** A dimension of Hans Eysenck's personality theory.

**longitudinal** Research that is conducted over an extended period of time.

**maladjusted tendencies** The development of behaviours that are antisocial and destructive.

**malignant tendencies** The development of behaviours that are not only antisocial but may cause deliberate harm to others.

**menarche** The appearance in females of the first menstrual period.

**neuroticism/stability** Another dimension of Hans Eysenck's personality theory.

**nomothetic** An approach which concentrates on the underlying priniciples of behaviour that can be generalised to whole populations.

**Oedipal complex** A Freudian term used to explain the problem facing a child in the phallic stage of psychosexual development, whereby the child must overcome his/her attachment to the opposite-sex parent and identify with the parent of the same sex.

**orthogonal scale** This is where two continuums are placed at right angles to each other so that a person may score on both at the same time.

**penis envy** During the resolution of the Oedipal complex a female realises she has no penis and feels envy towards males who have one.

**pleasure principle** That which the id works on, which is to seek out pleasure and avoid pain.

**pituitary gland** The 'master gland' of the endocrine system that regulates the actions of other endocrine glands.

**primary process** Freudian process that leads from unconscious need or desire to drive and behaviour.

**primary sexual changes** A variety of physical changes that occur during adolescence related to the ability to reproduce.

**premature foreclosure** According to Erikson this is when a young person makes their life choices too soon and risks an identity crisis in later life.

**pro-social behaviour** Social behaviours that are cooperative in nature.

**psychohistory** A research technique devised and used by Erikson, whereby he applied the principles of his whole life theory to major historical figures.

**psychological androgyny** This is where a sense of masculinity and femininity coexist within the same person.

**psychometric** Measuring an aspect of behaviour quantitatively.

**psychosexual stages** In Freud's theory these are the stages that children pass through on their way to sexual maturity.

**psychosocial moratorium** To delay the onset of adulthood.

**psychoticism** The third and final dimension of Hans Eysenck's personality theory, added at a later date.

**puberty** The period of physical development that occurs during adolescence whereby the individual matures sexually.

**optimal time periods** Periods of time during which certain problems etc. must be resolved if the best outcome is to be achieved.

**reality principle** This is the principle of the ego and simply means that although it will attempt to satisfy the needs of the id, it will only do so realistically, in terms of what is possible and what is not in the conscious world.

**reciprocal determinism** The idea that the situation we are in affects the way we behave, and in turn the way we behave affects the situation we are in.

**repudiation** This is where the adolescent withdraws from the adult world, and casts aside any thoughts of achieving an identity.

**rites of passage** The traditional rituals or accomplishments that help distinguish the adult from the child.

**secondary process** According to Freud, this is when the conscious part of the mind, which is linked to reality through the senses, begins to search for ways of satisfying the needs of the id.

**secondary sexual changes** Physical changes that take place during adolescence not related to the ability to reproduce. For example, deepening of the voice in males, changes in body shape, etc.

**self-efficacy** Linked to self-esteem but specifically our belief in our ability to overcome a problem we are facing.

**self-esteem** How we evaluate ourselves as people in terms of our belief in ourselves, our abilities, and our general worthiness.

**self-fulfilling prophesy** A term used to refer to the fact that what one expects to happen often turns out to be the case. For example, a student who expects to fail an exam will often act in ways that increase the likelihood of failure, such as not revising, thus fulfilling the original prophesy.

**sex role stereotypes** The separate roles expected of males and females.

**sex typing** A process of socialisation that takes account of the separate roles expected of males and females.

**socio-economic status** A rating of the status of an individual's position in society based on social and economic factors such as: family background, education, occupation, etc.

**social learning theory** A theory of learning that puts forward the view that learned behaviour comes about from observation and is mediated by cognitive variables.

**social model** An individual who is part of an experiment and plays a specific role.

**socially desirable** Behaviour or language that is seen as positive according to social/cultural norms.

**spermarche** In males the first ejaculation of sperm from the penis.

**superego** According to Freud this is the part of personality that acts like a social conscience.

**testicular feminization syndrome** A genetic abnormality whereby the male foetus is insensitive to the effects of male sex hormones and develops female external genitalia.

**test-retest reliability** To test the reliability of a questionnaire by administering the test twice to the same group of people, with an interval of time (e.g. one week) between the two administrations.

**unconscious** Not being aware of either external or internal events.

**validity** In relation to psychometric tests this refers to whether the tests are testing what they claim to be testing.

# References

Allport, G.W. (1961) *Pattern and growth in personality*. New York: Holt Rinehart Winston.

Allport, G.W. and Odbert, H.S. (1936) Trait names: a psychological-lexical study. *General and applied psychology* 47 (1, whole no. 211).

American Psychiatric Association (1994) *Diagnostic and statistical manual of mental disorders* (fourth edition). Washington, DC: Author.

Bailey, J., Bobrow, D., Wolfe, M. and Mikach, S. (1995) Sexual orientation of adult sons of gay fathers. Special Issue: Sexual orientation and human development. *Developmental Psychology* 31, 124–129.

Baker, D.P. and Jones, D.P. (1992) Opportunity and performance: a sociological explanation of gender differences in academic mathematics. In J. Wrigley (ed.), *Education and gender equality*. London: The Falmer Press.

Baldwin, W. and Cain, V.S. (1980) The children of teenage parents. *Family Planning Perspective* 12, 34–40.

Bandura, A. (1965) Influence of model's reinforcement contingencies on the acquisition of imitative responses. *Journal of Personality and Social Psychology* 1, 589–595.

Bandura, A. (1977) *Social Learning Theory* (second edition). Englewood Cliffs, NJ: Prentice-Hall.

Bandura, A. (1982) Self-efficacy mechanism in human agency. *American Psychologist* 37, 122–147.

Bandura, A., Ross, D. and Ross, S.A. (1961) Transmission of aggression through imitation of aggressive models. *Journal of Abnormal and Social Psychology* 63, 575–582.

Bandura, A., Ross, D. and Ross, S.A. (1963) Imitation of film-mediated aggressive models. *Journal of Abnormal and Social Psychology* 66, 3–11.

Barlow, D.H. and Durand, V.M. (1995) *Abnormal Psychology: an integrated approach*. New York: Brooks/Cole.

Baron, R.A. (1977) *Human Aggression*. New York: Plenum.

Barrett, P.T. and Kline, P. (1982) The itemetric properties of the Eysenck personality questionnaire: a reply to Helmes. *Personality and Individual Differences* 3, 73–80.

Belsky, J., Steinberg, L. and Draper, P. (1991) Childhood experience, interpersonal development, and reproductive strategy: an evolutionary theory of socialization. *Child Development* 62, 647–670.

Bem, S.L. (1974) The measurement of psychological androgeny. *Journal of Consulting and Clinical Psychology* 42, 155–162.

Bem, S.L. (1981) Gender Schema Theory: a cognitive account of sex typing. *Psychological Review* 88, 354–364.

Ben-Tovim, M.V. and Crisp, A. H. (1979) Personality and mental state within anorexia nervosa. *Journal of Psychosomatic Research* 23, 321–325.

Benokraitis, N.V. (1996) *Marriages and families: changes, choices, and constraints* (second edition). Upper Saddle River, NJ: Prentice-Hall.

Berk, L.E. (1997) *Child Development*. Chicago: Illinois State University Press.

Berman, P.W. and Jobes, D.A. (1991) *Adolescent suicide: assessment and intervention*. Washington, DC: American Psychological Association.

Berndt, T.J. (1979) Developmental changes in conformity to peers and parents. *Developmental Psychology* 15, 608–616.

Berscheid, E., Walster, E. and Bohrnstedt, G. (1973) The happy American body: a survey report. *Psychology Today* (June), 119–131.

Bowlby, J. (1973) *Attachment and Loss, Volume 2: Separation, Anxiety and Anger*. Harmondsworth: Penguin.

Brazzell, J.F. and Acock, A.C. (1988) Understanding attitudes, significant others, and aspirations on how adolescents intend to resolve a premarital pregnancy. *Journal of Marriage and Family* 50, 413–425.

Bridges, J.S. (1989) Sex differences in occupational values. *Sex Roles* 20 (3/4) 205–211.

Brooks-Gunn, J. and Ruble, D.N. (1984) The experience of menarche from a developmental perspective. In J.C. Brooks-Gunn and A.C. Peterson (eds), *Girls at puberty: biological, psychological and social perspectives*. New York: Plenum.

Brooks-Gunn, J. and Warren, W.P. (1988) The effects of delayed menarche in different contexts: dance and nondance students. *Journal of Youth and Adolescence* 14, 285–300.

Broverman, I.K., Vogel, S.R., Broverman, D.M., Clarkson, F.E. and Rosenkrantz, P. S. (1972) Sex role stereotypes: a current appraisal. *Journal of Social Issues* 28, 59–78.

Brozan, N. (1985) 'U.S. leads industrialized nations in teenage births and abortions.' *New York Times*, March 13, p.1. 105.

Burton, L.M. (1990) Teenage childbearing as an alternative life-course strategy in multigenerational black families. *Human Nature* 2, 163–176.

Byrnes, J.P. and Takahira, S. (1993) Explaining differences on the SAT-Math items. *Developmental Psychology* 29, 805–810.

Carson, R.C. and Butcher, J.N. (1992) Abnormal psychology and modern life (ninth edition). New York: Harper Collins.

Charlton, A. (1998) 'TV violence has little influence on children, study finds.' *The Times*, 12 January, p. 5.

Claridge, G.S. (1967) *Personality and arousal*. Oxford: Pergamon Press.

Clausen, J.A. (1975) The social meaning of differential physical maturation. In S.E. Dragastin and G.H. Elder (eds), *Adolescence in the life cycle*. New York: Halstead Press.

Clausen, J.A. (1995) The social meaning of differential physical and sexual maturation. In S.E. Dragastin and G.H. Elder Jr. (eds), *Adolescence in the life cycle*. New York: Halstead Press.

Cole, M. (1992) Culture in development. In M.H. Bornstein and M.E. Lamb (eds) *Developmental Psychology: an advanced textbook*. Hillsdale NJ: Lawrence Erlbaum Associates.

Coleman, J.C. (1974) *Relationships in adolescence*. London: Routledge & Kegan Paul.

Coleman, J.C. and Hendry, L. (1990) *The nature of adolescence* (second edition). London: Routledge.

Cooper, P.J. (1994) Eating disorders. In A.M. Colman (ed.) *Companion encyclopaedia of psychology*, Vol. 2. London: Routledge.

Comstock, G. and Paik, H. (1991) *Television and the American child*. San Diego: Academic Press.

Costa, P.T. and McCrae, R.R. (1993) Bullish on personality psychology. *The Psychologist: Bulletin of the British Psychological Society* 6 (7), 302–303.

Crystal, D.S., Chen, C., Fuligni, A.J., Stevenson, H.W., Hsu, C., Ko, H., Kitamura, S. and Kimura, S. (1994) Psychological maladjustment and academic achievement: a cross-cultural study of Japanese, Chinese and American high-school students. *Child Development* 65, 738–753.

Cumberbatch, G. (1990) *Television advertising and sex role stereotyping: a content analysis*. (Working paper IV for Broadcasting Standards Council). Communications Research Group, Aston University.

Damon, W. and Hart, D. (1988) *Self-understanding in childhood and adolescence*. New York: Cambridge University Press.

Dash, L. (1989) *When children want children*. New York: William and Morrow Company Inc.

Daubman, K., Heatherington, L. and Ahn, A. (1992) Gender and the self-presentation of academic achievement. *Sex Roles* 27, 187–204.

Deaux, K. (1985) Sex and gender. *Annual Review of Psychology* 36, 49–81.

DeRosier, M. and Kupersmidt, J.B. (1991) Costa Rican children's perceptions of their social networks. *Developmental Psychology* 27, 656–662.

Dimitrovsky, L., Perez-Hirshberg, M. and Itsokowitz, R. (1987) Depression during and following pregnancy: quality of family relationships. *Journal of Psychology* 121(3), 213–218.

Dimitrovsky, L., Singer, J. and Yinon, Y. (1989) Masculine and feminine traits: their relationship to suitedness for and success in training for traditionally masculine and feminine army functions. *Journal of Personality and Social Psychology* 57, 839–847.

Dishion, T.J., Patterson, G.R., Stoolmiller, M. and Skinner, M.L. (1991) Family, school and behavioural antecedents of early adolescent involvement with antisocial peers. *Developmental Psychology* 27, 172–180.

DoH (1992) *The Health of the Nation*. London: HMSO.

Dreyer, P.H. (1982) Sexuality during adolescence. In B. B. Wolman (ed.), *Handbook of Developmental Psychology*. New York: Wiley.

Dubow, E.F., Kausch, D.F., Blum, M.C., Reed, J. and Bush, E. (1989) Correlates of suicidal ideation and attempts in a sample of junior-high and high-school students. *Journal of Clinical Child Psychology* 18, 158–166.

Eagley, A.H. (1987) *Sex differences in social behaviour: a social-role interpretation*. Hillsdale, NJ: Lawrence Erlbaum Associates.

Eagley, A.H. and Steffen, V.J. (1986) Gender and aggressive behaviour: a meta-analytic review of the social psychological literature. *Psychological Bulletin* 100, 309–330.

Elias, J. and Gebhard, P. (1969) Sexuality and sexual learning in childhood. *Phi Delta Kappa* 50, 401–405.

Erikson, E.H. (1950) *Childhood and Society*. New York: Norton.

Erikson, E.H. (1968) *Identity: Youth and Crisis*. New York: Norton.

Erikson, E.H. (1969) *Gandhi's truth: on the origin of militant nonviolence*. New York: Norton.

Eron, L.D. (1982) Parent-child interaction, television violence, and aggression of children. *American Psychologist* 37, 197–211.

Eysenck, H.J. (1947) *Dimensions of Personality*. London: Routledge & Kegan Paul.

Eysenck, H.J. (1952) The Effects of Psychotherapy: An evaluation. *Journal of Consulting Psychology* 16, 319–324.

Eysenck, H.J. and Eysenck, M.W. (1985) *Personality and individual differences: a natural science approach*. New York: Plenum.

Eysenck, H.W. and Eysenck, S.B.G. (1964) *Manual of the Eysenck Personality Inventory*. London: University of London Press.

Eysenck, H.W. and Eysenck, S.B.G. (1975) *Manual for the Eysenck Personality Questionnaire*. London: Hodder & Stoughton.

Fagot, B.I. (1973) Sex-related stereotyping of toddlers' behaviour. *Developmental Psychology* 9, 429.

Fagot, B.I. (1978) The influence of sex of child on parental reactions to toddler children. *Child Development* 49, 459–465.

Fagot, B.I. and Leinbach, M.D. (1987) Socialization of sex roles within the family. In D.B. Carter (ed.), *Current conceptions of sex roles and sex typing: theory and research*. New York: Praeger.

Feingold, A. (1988) Cognitive gender differences are disappearing. *American Psychologist* 43, 95–103.

Feingold, A. (1992) Sex differences in variability in intellectual abilities: a new look at an old controversy. *Review of Educational Research* 62, 61–84.

Frable, D.E.S. (1989) Sex typing and gender ideology: two facets of the individual's gender psychology that go together. *Journal of Personality and Social Psychology* 56, 95–108.

Frable, D.E.S. and Bem, S.L. (1985) If you are gender schematic, all members of the opposite sex look alike. *Journal of Personality and Social Psychology* 49, 459–468.

Freeman, D. (1983) *Margaret Mead and the heretic: the making and unmaking of an anthropological myth*. Ringwood, Vic.: Penguin.

Freud, A. (1936) *The Ego and the Mechanisms of Defence*. London: Chatto & Windus.

Freud, A. (1969) *The Writings of Anna Freud*, Vol. 5 (Research at the Hampstead Child Therapy Clinic and Other Papers: 1956–1965.) New York: International Universities Press, Inc.

Freud, S. (1922) *Postscript (to the case of little Hans)*. Pelican Freud Library (8), Harmondsworth: Penguin.

Freud, S. (1933) *New Introductory Lectures on Psychoanalysis*. London: Hogarth Press.

Freud, S. (1976) [1901] *The Psychopathology of Everyday Life*. Pelican Freud Library (5), Harmondsworth: Penguin.

Freud, S. (1977) [1905] *Three Essays on the Theory of Sexuality*. Pelican Freud Library (7), Harmondsworth: Penguin.

Fromm, E. (1970) *The Crisis in Psychoanalysis*. Harmondsworth: Penguin.

Furnham, A. (1981) Personality and activity preference. *British Journal of Social Psychology* 20, 57–68.

Furstenberg, F.F. Jr, Brooks-Gunn, J. and Morgan, S.P. (1987) *Adolescent mothers in later life*. New York: Cambridge Press.

Gale, A. (1981) EEG studies of extraversion-introversion: what's the next step? In H.B. Gibson (ed.), *Hans Eysenck: The man and His Work*. London: Peter Owen.

Garland, A. and Zigler, E. (1993) Adolescent suicide prevention: current research and social policy implications. *American Psychologist* 48, 169–182.

Gibson, J. (1976) *Psychology for the Classroom*. Englewood Clifs, NJ: Prentice-Hall.

Girard, C. (1993) Age, gender and suicide: a cross-national analysis. *American Sociological Review* 58, 553–574.

Goodnow, J.J. (1996) From household practices to parents' ideas about work and interpersonal relationships. In S. Harkness and C. Super (eds), *Parents' cultural belief systems*. New York: Guilford Press.

Gough, H.G. (1952) Identifying psychological femininity. *Educational and Psychological Measurement* 12, 427–439.

Gould, S.J. (1981) *The Mismeasure of Man*. London: Penguin.

Gross, R.D. (1990) *Key Studies in Psychology* (second edition). London: Hodder & Stoughton.

Guisinger, S. and Blatt, S.J. (1994) Individuality and relatedness: evolution of fundamental dialect. *American Psychologist* 49, 104–111.

Gullotta, T.P., Adams, G.R. and Alexander, S.J. (1986) *Today's marriages and families. A wellness approach*. Monterey, CA: Brooks/Cole.

Hall, G. S. (1904) *Adolescence*. New York: Appleton & Co.

Hampson, S.E. (1995) The construction of personality. In S.E. Hampson and A. M. Colman (eds), *Individual Differences and Personality*. London: Longman.

Harkness, S. and Super, C. (1995) Culture and parenting. In M. Bornstein (ed.), *Handbook of Parenting*, Vol. 2. Hillsdale, NJ: Lawrence Erlbaum Associates.

Hartup, W.W. (1983) Peer relations. In P.H. Mussen (ed.), *Handbook of Child Psychology*, Vol. 4: Socialization, personality and social development. New York: Wiley.

Heatherington, T.F., Mahamedi, F., Striepe, M., Field, A.E. and Keel, P. (1997) A 10-year longitudinal study of body weight, dieting and eating disorder symptoms. *Journal of Abnormal Psychology* 106, 117–125.

Heim, A. (1970) *Intelligence and personality – their assessment and relationship*. Harmondsworth: Penguin.

Helman, C.G. (1990) *Culture, Health and Illness*. London: Butterworth.

Herman-Giddens, M.E., Slora, E.J., Wasserman, A.C., Bourdony, C.J., Bhapkar, M.V., Koch G.G. and Hasemeie, C.M. (1997) Secondary sexual characteristics and menses in young girls seen in office practise: a study from the pediatric research office settings network. *Pediatrics* 99, 505–512.

Hetherington, E.M. and Parke, R.D. (1999) *Child Psychology: A Contemporary Viewpoint* (fifth edition). Boston: McGraw Hill College.

Hines, M. (1993) Hormonal and neural correlates of sex-typed behavioural development in human beings. In M. Haug, R.E. Whalen, C. Aron and K.L. Olson (eds), *The development of sex differences and similarities in behaviour*. Boston: Kluwer.

Holt, R.R. (1967) Individuality and generalization in the psychology of personality. In R.S. Lazarus and E.M. Opton (eds), *Personality*. Harmondsworth: Penguin.

Holtzman, W.H., Diaz-Guerrero, R. and Schwartz, J.D. (1975) *Personality development in two cultures: cross-cultural and longitudinal study of school children in Mexico and the United States*. Austin: University of Texas Press.

Huesman, L.R. and Eron, L.D. (1986) *Television and the aggressive child: a cross-national comparison*. Hillsdale, NJ: Lawrence Erlbaum Associates.

Huston, A.C. (1983) Sex-typing. In P.H. Mussen (ed.), *Handbook of Child Psychology*, Vol. 4: Socialization, personality and social development. New York: Wiley.

Jacklin, C.N. (1989) Male and female: issues of gender. *American Psychologist* 44, 127–133.

Jonides, J. and Rozin, P. (1981) *Study guide for Gleitman's basic psychology*. New York: Norton.

Jung, C.G. (1913) The theory of psycho-analysis. *Journal of Psychoanalysis* 5, 307–315.

Kahn, S., Zimmerman, G., Csikszentmihaly, M. and Getzels, J.W. (1985) Relations between identity in young adulthood and intimacy at midlife. *Journal of Personality and Social Psychology* 49, 1316–1322.

Kendrick, D.C. (1981) Neuroticism and extraversion as explanatory concepts in clinical psychology. In H.B. Gibson (ed.), *Hans Eysenck: The man and His Work*. London: Peter Owen.

Kerns, K.A. and Berenbaum, S.A. (1991) Sex differences in spatial ability in children. *Behaviour Genetics* 21, 383–396.

Kirkby, R. and Radford, J. (1976) *Individual differences*. London: Methuen.

Kline, P. (1989) Objective tests of Freud's theories. In A.M. Colman and J.G. Beaumont (eds), *Psychology Survey* No.7. Leicester: British Psychological Society.

Kluckhohn, C. and Murray, H.A. (1953) Personality formation: the determinants. In C. Kluckhohn, H.A. Murray and D.M. Schneider (eds), *Personality in nature, society and culture* (second edition). New York: Knopf.

Kohlberg, L.A. (1966) A cognitive-developmental analysis of children's sex-role concepts and attitudes. In E.E. Maccoby (ed.), *The development of sex differences*. Stanford, CA: Stanford University Press.

Kroger, J. (1985) Separation-individuation and ego-identity status in New Zealand university students. *Journal of Youth and Adolescence* 14, 133–147.

Lader, M. (1975) *The Psychophysiology of Mental Illness*. London: Routledge & Kegan Paul.

Levinger, G. and Clark, J. (1961) Emotional factors in the forgetting of word associations. *Journal of Abnormal and Social Psychology* 62, 99–105.

Lewis, M. and Rosenbum, M.A. (1975) *Friendship and peer relations*. New York: Wiley.

Loehlin, J.C., Willerman, L. and Horn, J.M. (1988) Human behaviour genetics. *Annual Review of Psychology* 39, 101–133.

Maccoby, E.E. (1980) *Social Development: psychological growth and the parent-child relationship*. New York: Harcourt Brace Jovanovich.

Maccoby, E.E. (1990) Gender and relationships: a developmental account. *American Psychologist* 45, 513–521.

Maccoby, E.E. and Jacklin, C.N. (1974) *The Psychology of Sex Differences*. Stanford, CA: Stanford University Press.

McCrae, R.R. and Costa, P.T. (1987) Validation of the five factor model of personality across instruments and observers. *Journal of Personality and Social Psychology* 52, 81–90.

McKnight, C.C, Crosswhite, F.J., Dossey, J.A., Kifer, E., Swafford, J.O., Travers, K.J. and Cooney, T.J. (1987) *The underachieving curriculum. Assessing US school mathematics from an international perspective*. Champaign, IL:Stipes.

Malcolm, L.A. (1970) Growth of the Asai child of the Madang district of New Guinea. *Journal of Biosocial Science* 2, 213–226.

Marcia, J.E. (1966) Development and validation of ego-identity status. *Journal of Personality and Social Psychology* 3, 551–558.

Marcia, J.E. (1967) Ego-identity status: relationship to change in self esteem, general maladjustment and authoritarianism. *Journal of Personality* 35, 118–133.

Marcia, J.E. (1976) Identity six years after: a follow-up study. *Journal of Youth and Adolescence* 5, 145–160.

Marsh, H.W. (1989) Age and sex effects in multiple dimensions of self-concept: a replication and extension. *Australian Journal of Psychology* 37, 197–204.

Marsiglio, W. and Menaghan, E. (1990) Pregnancy resolution and family formation: understanding gender differences in adolescents' preferences and beliefs. *Journal of Family Issues* 11, 313–333.

Martin, C.L. and Halverson, C.F. Jr (1981) A schematic processing model of sex-typing and stereotyping in children. *Child Development* 52, 1119–1134.

Martin, C.L. and Halverson, C.F. Jr (1983) The effects of sex-typing schemas on young children's memory. *Child Development* 54, 563–574.

Martin, C.L. and Halverson, C.F. Jr (1987) The roles of cognition in sex-roles and sex-typing. In D. B. Carter (ed.), *Current conceptions of sex-roles and sex-typing: theory and research*. New York: Praeger.

Martorell, R., Mendoza, F.S., Baisden, K. and Pawson, R.G. (1994) Physical growth, sexual maturation and obesity in Puerto Rican children. In G. Lamberty and C.G. Coll (eds), *Puerto Rican women and children: issues in health, growth and development*. New York: Plenum.

Masterson, J.F. (1967) *The Psychiatric Dilemma of Adolescence*. Boston, MA: Little, Brown.

Mead, M. (1931) *Growing up in New Guinea*. London: George Routledge and Sons Ltd.

Mead, M. (1935) *Sex and Temperament in Three Primitive Societies*, London: Routledge & Kegan Paul.

Mead, M. (1965) *Coming of Age in Samoa. A study of adolescence and sex in primitive societies*. London: Penguin.

Meeker, B. F. and Weitzel-O'Neill, P. A. (1977) Sex roles and inter-personal behaviour in task-oriented groups. *American Sociological Review* 42, 91–104.

Meilman, P.W. (1979) Cross-sectional age changes in ego identity status during adolescence. *Developmental Psychology* 15, 230–231.

Mischel, W. (1968) *Personality and Assessment*. New York: Wiley.

Mischel, W. (1976) Introduction of Personality (second edition). New York: Holt, Rinehart & Winston.

Moffitt, T.E., Caspi, A., Belsky, J. and Silva, P.A. (1992) Childhood experience and the onset of menarche: a test of a sociobiological model. *Child Development* 63, 47–58.

Money, J. (1985) Pediatric sexology and hermaphrodism. *Journal of Sex and Marital Therapy* 11, 139–156.

Money, J. (1987) Sin, Sickness or Status? Homosexual gender identity and psychoneuroendocrinology. *American Psychologist* 42, 384–399.

Money, J. and Ehrhardt, A. (1972) *Man and woman, boy and girl.* Baltimore: Johns Hopkins University Press.

Money, J. and Tucker, P. (1975) *Sexual signatures: On being a man or a woman.* Boston, MA: Little, Brown.

Moore, S. and Rosenthal, D. (1992) *Sexuality in Adolescence.* London: Routledge.

Morrison, D.M. (1985) Adolescent contraceptive behaviour: a review. *Psychological Bulletin* 98, 538–568.

Offer, D., Ostrov, E., Howard, K.I. and Atkinson, R. (1988) *The Teenage World: Adolescents' Self-image in Ten Countries.* New York: Plenum.

Patterson, C. J. (1992) Children of gay and lesbian parents. *Child Development* 63, 1025–1042.

Perry, D.C. and Bussey, K. (1979) The social learning theory of sex differences: imitation is live and well. *Journal of Personality and Social Psychology* 37, 1699–1712.

Perry, D.G., White, A.J. and Perry, L.C. (1984) Does early sex-typing result in children's attempts to match their behaviour to sex role stereotypes? *Child Development* 55, 2114–2121.

Phoenix, A. (1991) *Young Mothers?* Cambridge: Polity Press.

Piran, N., Kennedy, S., Garfinkel, P.E. and Owens, M. (1985) Affective disturbance in eating disorders. *Journal of Nervous and Mental Disease* 173, 395–400.

Pomerleau, A., Bolduc, D., Malcuit, G. and Cossette, L. (1990) Pink or blue: environmental gender stereotypes in the first two years of life. *Sex Roles* 22, 359–367.

Popper, K. (1959) *The Logic of Scientific Discovery.* London: Routledge & Kegan Paul.

Radford, J. and Kirby, R. (1975) *The Person in Psychology.* London: Methuen.

Reid, P.T., Tate, C.S. and Berman, P.W. (1989) Pre-school children's self presentations in situations with infants: effects of sex and race. *Child Development* 60, 710–714.

Richards, M.H., Boxer, A.M., Petersen, A.C. and Albrecht, R. (1990) Relation of weight to body image in pubertal girls and boys from two communities. *Developmental Psychology* 26, 313–321.

Roche, A.F. (1979) (ed.) *Secular trends: human growth, maturation and development*. Monographs of the Society for Research in Child Development, 44 (serial No. 179).

Rogers, C.T. (1951) *Client-centred Therapy*. Boston, MA: Houghton Mifflin.

Rosen, R. and Hall, E. (1984) *Sexuality*. New York: Random House.

Rubin, K.H., Bukowski, W. and Parker, J.G. (1998) Peer interactions, relationships, and groups. In W. Damon (gen. ed.) and N. Eisenberg (vol. ed.), *Handbook of Child Psychology*, Vol. 3. Social, emotional and personality development (fifth edition). New York: Wiley.

Ruble, D.N. and Martin, C. L. (1998) Gender development. In W. Damon (gen. ed.) and N. Eisenberg (vol. ed), *Handbook of Child Psychology* Vol. 3. New York: Wiley.

Rutter, M. (1976) Sex differences in children's responses to family stress. In E.J. Anthony and C.M. Konpernick (eds), *The child in his family*. New York:Wiley.

Ryff, C.D. and Heinke, S.G. (1983) Subjective organisation of personality in adulthood and ageing. *Journal of Personality and Social Psychology* 44, 807–816.

Sebald, H. (1986) Adolesecents' shifting orientation toward parents and peers: a curvilinear trend over recent decades. *Journal of Marriage and the Family* 48, 5–13.

Shankman, D. (1996) The history of Somoan sexual conduct and the Mead–Freeman controversy. *American Anthropologist* 98(3), 555–567.

Sherman, J.A. (1983) Girls talk about mathematics and their future: a partial replication. *Psychology of Women Quarterly* 7, 338–342.

Shields, J. (1976) Heredity and environment. In H.J. Eysenck and D.G. Wilson (eds), *Textbook of Human Psychology*. Lancaster: MTP.

Simmons, R. and Blyth, D.A. (1987) *Moving into Adolescence: the impact of pubertal change and school context*. Hawthorne, NY: Aldine de Gruyter.

Skelton, G. (1990) 'As women climb political ladder, stereotypes follow.' *Los Angeles Times*, pp. A1, A24–A25.

Smith, K. and Crawford, S. (1986) Suicidal behaviour among 'normal' high school students. *Suicide and Life-Threatening Behaviour* 16, 313–325.

Spearman, C. (1904) General intelligence, objectively determined and measured. *American Journal of Psychology* 15, 201–293.

Spender, D. (1983) *Invisible Women: Schooling Scandal.* London: Women's Press.

Stagnor, C. and Ruble, D.N. (1987) Development of gender role knowledge and gender constancy. In L.S. Liben and M.L. Signorella (eds), *Children's gender schemata: new directions for child development.* San Francisco: Jossey-Bass.

Steinberg, L. (1987) Impact of puberty on family relations: effects of pubertal status and pubertal timing. *Developmental Psychology* 23, 451–460.

Steinberg, L. and Silverberg, S.B. (1986) The visicitudes of autonomy in early adolescence. *Child Development* 57, 841–851.

Stevens, R. (1995) Freudian theories of personality. In S.E. Hampson and A. M. Colman (eds), *Individual differences and personality.* London: Longman.

Stevenson, H.W., Lee, S.Y. and Stigler, J.W. (1986) Mathematics achievement of Chinese, Japanese and American children. *Science* 231, 693–699.

Stevenson, H.W. and Lee, S.Y. (1990) *Contexts of achievement. A study of American, Chinese and Japanese children.* Monographs of the Society for Research in Child Development, 55 (1–2 serial no. 221).

Stevenson, H.W., Chen, C. and Lee, S. (1993) Mathematics achievement of Chinese, Japanese and American children: ten years later. *Science* 259, 53–58.

Strong, E.K. (1943) *Vocational Interest of Men and Women.* Stanford, CA: Stanford University Press.

Tanner, J.M. (1990) *Fetus into man: physical growth from conception to maturity.* Cambridge, MA: Harvard University Press.

Turner, P.J. and Gervai, J. (1995) A multidimensional study of gender typing in pre-school children and their parents: personality, attitudes, preferences, behaviour and cultural differences. *Developmental Psychology* 31, 759–772.

Urlberg, K.A., Degirmencioglu, S.M., Tolson, J.M. and Halliday-Scher, K. (1995) The structure of adolescent peer networks. *Developmental Psychology* 31 (4), 540–547.

Voydanoff, P. and Donnelly, B. (1991) Attitudes towards pregnancy resolutions among adolescent women. *Family Perspective* 25, 163–178.

Waterman, A.S. (1982) Identity development from adolescence

to adulthood: an extension of theory and review of research. *Developmental Psychology* 18, 341 358.

Weinraub, M., Clemens, L.P., Sockloff, A., Ethridge, T., Graceley, E. and Myers, B. (1984) The development of sex-role stereotypes in the third year: relationships to gender labelling, gender identity, sex-typed toy preference and family characteristics. *Child Development* 55, 1493–1503.

Weisner, T.S. and Wilson-Mitchell, J.E. (1990) Nonconventional family lifestyles and multischematic sex typing in six year olds. *Child Development* 61, 1915–1933.

Weitzman, N., Birns, B. and Friend, R. (1985) Traditional and non-traditional mothers' communication with their daughters and sons. *Child Development* 56, 894–898.

Wierson, M., Long, P.J. and Forehand, R.L. (1993) Toward a new understanding of early menarche: the role of environmental stress in pubertal timing. *Adolescence* 28, 913–924.

Wilkinson, F.R. and Cargill, D.W. (1955) Repression elicited by story material based on the Oedipal complex. *Journal of Social Psychology* 42, 209–14.

Wrightsman, L.S. (1977) *Social Psychology* (second edition). Monterey, CA: Brooks/Cole.

Youniss, J. and Smollar, J. (1985) *Adolescent relations with mothers, fathers and friends*. Chicago: University of Chicago Press.

Zuckerman, M. (1991) *Psychobiology of Personality*. Cambridge: Cambridge University Press.

# Index